M000110834

The Experts Praise
Managing Your Business Data

This is the best book about data that I have ever read. It is incredibly insightful, and it explains—in terms that can be understood by the business—what data is and what are the issues, challenges and solutions around it. It is a must-read for every business executive who wants to understand and use data in their organization. A much-needed and ground-breaking book in the Information Management industry.

>Alicia G. Acebo
>Principal
>RockPaperData.com

Managing Your Business Data demonstrates the authors' actionable experience in instilling a data-driven culture from boardroom to cubicle to data centers in today's corporations. But this is not just meant for the data geeks among us but also for the business leaders: for example, how to balance "gut" versus numbers (the six steps to trusting your data). To jumpstart your company's data evolution, you need to focus on the right data stage and the author's show you "how to" by innovatively applying Maslow's Needs Hierarchy. But real achievement means driving lasting behavior change—not just technology and process: in here you'll find a roadmap for the six stages to optimizing data management. And, of course, you need metrics and KPIs to monitor your success: you'll soon be able to identify the 6 clues that your company's data behavior is changing positively. This is a real practitioner's guide whether you are a data professional, or in marketing, sales, business management, finance, or operations. It provides new perspectives as well as reinforcing lessons learned.

>Cathy Cooper
>Senior Director, Database Marketing
>Global Marketing Operations
>SAP

In this perceptive book, authors Theresa Kushner and Maria Villar deal with a problem that is common in many large organizations today: irreconcilable data. The Sale VP has his data, IT has data, Finance has data, Marketing has data and the new

CRM system has data—all concerning the same customers. The problem: the various sources of data do not agree. It is almost impossible to get them reconciled. Kushner and Villar's solution: a Chief Data Officer whose job it is to find out the reasons for the data problems and solve them. Step by step, they show how these differences in entering, counting, recording, categorizing and summarizing data can be resolved. A book like this has been badly needed by some of America's largest corporations. It is an "insider's" study of a common corporate problem that will be much appreciated by many parts of America's fortune 500 companies—in addition to thousands of smaller enterprises which have similar problems.

Arthur Middleton Hughes
Vice President / Solutions Architect
KnowledgeBase Marketing
Author *Strategic Database Marketing* 3rd Ed.

Spectacular depiction of how data transforms into insights and ultimately delivering real value to an organization. The authors do an outstanding job in explaining all of the critical elements for business intelligence to be successful. A must read whether you are in the business intelligence business for years or just starting this book offers kernels of wisdom for everyone!

Sheila Jordan
VP Information Technology, Communication and Collaboration
Cisco Systems.

I've done extensive reading to develop best practices in the areas of customer intelligence, satisfaction, and loyalty, looking at what world-class companies are doing and how they're doing it. I wish Kushner and Villar's book had been available to me then, because it all comes down to the data you have, it's quality, and availability. This book provides invaluable information you need to convince executives of the importance of data management, managing data as an asset, and deploying a data management program. This is an outstanding read for anyone who needs a blueprint for how to tackle managing business data.

Mary E. Orr
Director, Strategic Sales & Marketing Support
ChoicePoint

Management of corporate data as an enterprise asset has long been the aspiration of innovators and data bigots alike. But few have recognized the importance of making this a top management issue as opposed to a technical challenge. Villar and Kushner have captured the essence of the issues and provide real life pragmatic advice and detailed guidelines that will help practitioners succeed.

Bernie Plagman, Chairman
TechPar Group, LLC

Data is power. Unmanaged, it is power underutilized and sometimes out of control. Managing Your Business Data in today's cyber world is critical to business success. Ms Kushner and Ms Villar have provided a valuable reference on what to do and how to do it. It's not exactly bedtime reading but it is an excellent volume to have next to your computer or on your office reference book shelf.

Peter J Rosenwald
Principal, Consult Partners
Founder and President of Wunderman Worldwide and
Former Chairman of Saatchi & Saatchi Direct
Author, *Accountable Marketing*.

In a globalized world, being competitive often means knowing more, being more accurate, visible or responsive than the others. Business data is at the core of this competitive advantage—data which increasingly comes from sources outside of your own business. Consequently, having a comprehensive master data management plan, organization and tools in place is becoming THE differentiation factor for forward looking businesses. This book provides a clear and concise roadmap for business leaders who wish to drive their operations ahead of the crowd.

John G. Schwarz
CEO
Business Objects

I am so happy that Theresa Kushner and Maria Villar took the time out of their busy schedules to share these insights with us. We marketers understand the importance of customer information in driving shareholder value, but we haven't been very effective at explaining to the rest of the organization how and why to capture, store, update and protect data. So this book provides a real service. I am especially keen on the section about Chapter 9, a step-by-step guide to deploying a data management program. Let's hope that organizations large and small take advantage of these practical instructions for success.

Ruth Stevens
President, eMarketing Strategy
Professor of Marketing
School of Business
Columbia University.

This is the kind of information people need to bridge the gap between IT thinking and business thinking. Should be required reading in management IT classes. Really does a great job of covering the basics people need to understand when applying technology to management situations.

Fits very well with Data-Driven Business Models for people who need a deeper technical focus. Fits very well with management IT curriculum for people who need more of a management focus.

Alan Weber
Principal, Owner, Data to Strategy Group LLC
Author, *Data-Driven Business Models*

MANAGING YOUR BUSINESS DATA

From Chaos to Confidence

THERESA KUSHNER
Cisco Systems

MARIA VILLAR
MCV LLC

RĀCM
COMMUNICATIONS

Chicago

Published by:

Racom Books
Racom Communications
150 N. Michigan ave.
Suite 2800
Chicago, IL 60601
312-494-0100
www.racombooks.com

Editor: Richard Hagle
Cover and interior design: Sans Serif, Inc.

ISBN: 978-1-933199-13-9

DEDICATION

Special thanks go to our families who sacrificed two years of missed dinners, family gatherings and other important events.

To Ben Villar, my husband, who always supports my goals and provided a business perspective I greatly valued while writing this book. [Maria Villar]

To Matthew and David Kushner who learned to live with a wife and mother who spent most weekends writing. [Theresa Kushner]

ACKNOWLEDGMENTS

Three executives occupied the backseat of the stretch limo headed to New Jersey from White Plains on that clear October day—Maria Villar, myself and Harris Warsaw, VP of Marketing for the sales division of IBM. For two years, Maria and I had worked closely managing data for marketing—she from the enterprise CIO's office, me from within marketing. That day we were on our way to meet with Dun & Bradstreet and forge a closer relationship between our two companies. For that, we needed Harris who was the IBM executive sponsor for D&B.

Harris is a rare executive—one that clearly understands how data can make or break his business and he put his beliefs to work by sponsoring a customer intelligence organization within marketing and supporting Maria's enterprise efforts. That day his belief in the power of data was all we needed. Maria and I jokingly said to him, "We need to write a book about data." And Harris enthusiastically seconded the idea, "You should call it 'It's All About the Data.'"

So here it is, Harris. It doesn't have that title, but it is all about the data. Thanks for believing in us.

There are others who also believed that this book needed to be written: Mary Orr from ChoicePoint who asked every month if it was ready yet; [John Schwarz of Business Object who offered customer insight and executive perspective along the way

And finally our deepest gratitude goes to Rich Hagle who believed in us even when this book didn't fit the usual category of books that he publishes.

CONTENTS

Preface   ix

SECTION I   **Why Should You Care About Data?**   1

1. **Data, Fact, and Your Gut**   3

   What Kind of Data Is Important?   4
   Basic Data Characteristics and Attributes   6
   Creating Effective Data   7
   How Do You Know to Trust the Data?   8
   Summary   10

2. **Data: The Key to a Complete View of Your Customer**   11

   Data and the 360-Degree View   11
   Obstacles to a 360-Degree View   13

3. **Data and Compliance**   16

   Compliance and Data Management   18
   Information Security and Risk Management   20
   Information Security Legislation and Standards   21
   Information Security and Data Management Implications   23
   Data Privacy Legislation and Standards   24
   Data Privacy and Data Management Implications   27
   Financial Reporting Legislation and Standards   28
   Financial Reporting and Data Implications   29
   Summary   30

4. **Data and Performance Measurement**   31

   What Is Business Performance Management (BPM) Anyway?   31
   What Makes a BPM Application Difficult?   33
   Data Challenges   33
   Twelve Steps to Making BPM Work   34
   Data Management Implications   42
   Summary   44

5. **Growing and Managing a Data Culture**   45

   A Hierarchy of Human Needs   45
   A Hierarchy of Data Needs   48

Implementing a Data Management Culture   54
Summary   55

SECTION II   **Making Data Work for You**   57

6. The Ballad of "Bad Data"   59

The Data's Bad!   59
Wally's Dilemma   60
The Ninety-day Project   62
Nine Months Later   62
It's Not Easy   63

7. Start at the Top: Putting Data Management on the Executive Agenda   65

Ways to Get Management Attention   68
Summary   73

8. Managing Data as a Company Asset   74

Asset Inventory   75
The Enterprise Metadata Repository   79
Who Should the Enterprise Metadata Owner Be?   80
The Benefits of Metadata   81
Obstacles to Creating an Enterprise Metadata Repository   83
Determining the Data Asset Value   85
Roles and Responsibilities   88
Policies and Procedures   89
Asset Management and Accountability   90
Summary   91

9. Deploying Enterprise Data Management in Stages   92

Addressing the Safety Needs of Reliability and Consistency   93
Addressing Data Quality   101
Three Myths of Data Quality   102
Who Is Responsible for Data Quality?   104
How Do You Manage Data Quality?   106
What Actions Should You Take to Ensure Ongoing Data Quality?   107
Where Should You Start a Data-quality Program?   108
Addressing Privacy and Security   110
Summary   112
For Further Reading   113

10. Establishing Accountability and Governance   114

Appointing a Data Leader   114
Why a Chief Data Officer for Your Firm?   115
What Are the Chief Data Officer's Responsibilities?   117
What Are the Skills and Characteristics of the CDO?   117

Who Should the Chief Data Officer Report to Within the Firm?   119
What Are Some Measurements of Success for the CDO?   121
Is the Chief Data Officer a Permanent Position?   121
Appointing Business Data Stewards   122
Why Do You Need a Business Data Steward?   122
How Should You Think About Business Data Stewards
    and Their Mission?   124
What Are the Attributes of an Effective Business Data Steward?   128
What Level Is the Business Data Steward and to Whom Does
    the Steward Report?   129
Getting Started with Limited Resources   130
How to Ensure a Successful Business Data Stewardship Program
    in Your Organization   130
Training the Business Data Steward   131
What Governance and Management Systems Should
    a Chief Data Officer Employ?   132
A Matrix Organization: Business Data Steward and
    Chief Data Officer   135
Assessing and Measuring Progress of Data Management Maturity   135
Data Management Scorecard   137
Summary   137
For More Information   138

11. **Get Talent: Securing the Right Data Skills**   139

Skills of the Information Management Professional   140
To Certify or Not to Certify?   142
Summary   143

12. **Communicate and Educate: Selling Data and Overcoming
    Resistance**   144

Changing Attitudes About Data   144
Dealing with Resistance—The Chief Data Officer's Challenge   147
Selling the Benefits of Data Management   149
Summary   154

Index   155

PREFACE

Chaos, a state of utter confusion or disorder; a total lack of organization.
Confidence, full trust; belief in the powers, trustworthiness, reliability.

Between these two states exists a gap of seemingly immeasurable distance. This is especially true if you find yourself confused about the basic information that should be helping you manage your business. Do you ever find yourself . . .

- Not trusting your sales achievements or forecasts?
- Having to restate your financials?
- Making decisions about acquisitions without really knowing how they will be assimilated into your organization?
- Managing transactions without the benefit of credit or financial information on your customers?
- Not feeling comfortable with your suppliers' invoices, your manufacturing production reports, your sales organization's territory analysis?
- In other words, **flying by the seat of your pants?**

Information chaos feels like this.

In our collective years in business, we have met a good many executives who felt uneasy about the data they saw and a good many more who never saw a number that they liked. What we found when we questioned them about this unease was that very few of them trusted the systems or processes that produced the reports they depended on. All it usually took was one number not being correct, one piece of information that didn't match their own experience and they began to mistrust everything. As a result, many of them would rather rely on their years of experience, their gut, their instinct than take a chance on a piece of information based on data that they just "knew" was incorrect. Some of these executive managers had developed great coping skills. They learned to mitigate their uncertainty by endless analyses and double-checking done by many people across the organization. Chaos, in these circumstances, often looks like work overload on the accounting and operations departments.

We set out in these 12 chapters to offer a beginning, a way for management to start looking at how to manage the data that they depend on without feeling that it was impossible, to mitigate that feeling of chaos. We wanted to help managers who want to depend on the numbers they see to understand that there is a way to organize data, manage it and use it that can lead to confidence and trust. As it turns out, it's not really that difficult, but it takes focus and determination. More importantly, it takes leaders who won't shy away from the complexity of the situation. It takes leadership that is willing to roll up its sleeves and dive into the details. In all the reading we've done about managing systems and implementing business intelligence programs, the one factor that often guarantees success is this leadership, a direction and desire from the top to tackle the issues.

We believe that the end result is *believing* in the reliability of your reports, trusting the data that helps you make business decisions. In other words, the end result is confidence. In these times of economic uncertainty, confidence cannot be minimized. It is at the heart of the American business psyche and worth protecting at all costs.

We sincerely hope that this book helps you in some small measure to restore your confidence.

SECTION I

Why Should You Care About Data?

Just do a Google search for the term "data." It returns 1,690,000,000 entries for everything from Data on *Star Trek: The Next Generation* to census data to math data. As a business person, you have more data to help you run your business than ever existed in human history. So why do you need a book on data? Why should you care?

Even with the great amount of data available to you, you might find that you have a love/hate relationship with it. You love it when it gives you good information about what markets to pursue or which competitors you've recently surpassed. But you hate it when you can't get the sales figures fast enough, or worse still, they don't reflect what you know to be reality.

This book was written for the executive who wants to understand the lifeblood of her company, the manager who wants to be able to make better decisions, the professional who knows that managing information is the best way to protect and grow a business. This book is designed to help you as a business leader think about the use of data and its impact on your daily operation. Equally important, this book will also help you understand the role you, as a business leader, play in ensuring the data meets your needs. Let's put it this way: If you are perfectly healthy, you may not think about such vital signs as blood pressure, cholesterol, body temperature or heart rate. But if you suddenly take ill or have an accident, those data points become extremely important to you. In your organization, the same is true. You may not pay much attention to the operational details of your business unless you suddenly miss a quarterly sales forecast, experience a competitor's predatory move, or have to manage a sudden drop in the market valuation of your stock. When your organization is growing, profitable and returning ever-increasing value to the shareholders, it's often difficult to concentrate on data issues that drive decision-making and measurements. In this situation, it takes insightful and forward-thinking management to aggressively monitor the vital signs of a healthy organization and look to the health of the data that creates its metrics. We are assuming that you represent the best of management today and do indeed want to stay healthy as an organization. For you, we offer only three reasons why you should care about data:

1. It helps you make better business decisions by *knowing your customers better.*
2. It helps you meet government and industry *regulations.*
3. It makes it possible to *measure* how well you made those decisions and consider mid-course corrections, if necessary.

You are exceptional in that you've already decided that understanding more about data will help you become a better business manager. Why else would you have bought this book? But you may be in the minority. Understanding data and all of its complexity is not one of the topics that business schools teach nor is it a topic that gets to the board room often. When it does make it there, it's usually not a good appearance. But understanding data, how it affects your business and how to participate in its management, can be one of the most important exercises you do to keep your business healthy and growing.

1

Data, Fact, and Your Gut

A bright, experienced Vice President of Sales at a large technology company looked around the room at the group of executives gathered in his conference room and frowned at the figures projected onto the screen at the end of the conference table. "I don't believe these numbers," he said, referring to the market research that had just been presented. "They don't agree with what I know about the marketplace." What followed this pronouncement was a flurry of questions regarding the integrity of the data presented.

How many times have you sat through similar presentations? The numbers tell a story, but no one believes the story. As a result, the numbers get the blame. This same vice president said quietly to his market research manager after the meeting: "I only do market research to confirm what I already feel."

Sadly, this vice president is not alone in his feelings about data and its applicability to the reality of running a business. The numbers of dollars are well understood, but the numbers of market research, customer satisfaction and a host of other data-based views of business life are constantly challenged. We are, after all, only human. We form opinions based on what we see, hear and read. And, often those opinions are, unfortunately, *not* based on facts or data. How else can you account for so many products and businesses that fail? Either these businesses had the data and failed to act on it or they didn't have the right data. Either way, most businesspeople today depend more on experience and gut feelings than on data and hard information.

In their book, *Your Gut is Still Not Smarter Than Your Head*, authors Kevin Clancy and Peter Krieg bemoan the fact that marketing executives are still embracing the idea of "thinking without thinking" and relate this fact to the reason why the "average CMO (Chief Marketing Officer) tenure is 23 months." Their own study on marketing decision-making in the summer of 2006 echoed these facts:

The majority of the 256 marketing executive respondents agreed with the statements, "I feel very confident making marketing decisions based on my own sense of what our customers will respond to" (66 percent); "Generally speaking, I tend to make decisions quickly based on my judgment and experi-

ence (62 percent); and "I agree with Malcolm Gladwell in his book Blink when he argues that senior marketing managers should rely more on intuition and judgment in making major decisions and avoid becoming mired in data" (53 percent).

Four out of 10 marketing executives openly admitted that "With the right people in place, companies can liberate themselves from their obsession with data-driven decisions" and "I rely more heavily on intuition and judgment than science in making marketing decisions."

Marketing executives, unfortunately, are not the only group that does not rely on the numbers or data. Gary Lillien and Arvind Rangaswamy, in their book *Marketing Engineering,* cite a 1989 study by Russo and Schoemaker that quantitatively points out subjective decision models are superior to mental models, but that formal, objective models do far better.

Mental models are those that you develop through years of experience. Stockbrokers, professors, doctors and businesspeople all have developed beliefs born of years of experience. These "truths" are their mental models. Subjective decision models are those that combine an element of those known "truths" with some data. The best example of this is a sales manager who accurately forecasts his quarterly sales by talking with each of his sales reps, gathering their inputs from a sales forecast system and then applying his own estimations of what might happen. His forecast is a combination of numbers and intuition. A completely objective model is one driven totally by data. In this case a sales manager would forecast his sales based on a forecasting model that uses five years of data and applies that knowledge to the entries made by his reps for this quarter.

In Exhibit 1.1, you see the summation of Russo and Schoemaker's work showing that using data to guide and inform a business decision helps you make a better decision. True, nothing will replace the human mind and the intuition that causes us to innovate and take chances, but data can help you narrow the risks of innovating too early or jumping at opportunities that may not be as good as you imagine.

What Kind of Data Is Important?

One of the most vexing questions that data managers and business intelligence analysts have to solve is what data is important to the business. They rely on business managers to help them answer these questions, but business managers think in terms of business objectives and outcomes, not in terms of data elements. Here you need to combine these two worlds—data and business—to understand what kind of data is more important. Approaching the question from both the business and the data side affords you a better view of considerations.

Start with the business objectives. Data that can materially affect a business objective such as:

Exhibit 1.1. Judgments Using Various Decision Models

Types of Judgments Experts Had to Make	Mental Model	Subjective Decision Model	Objective Decision Model
Academic performance of graduate students	.19	.25	.54
Life expectancy of cancer patients	-.01	.13	.35
Changes in stock prices	.23	.29	.80
Mental illness using personality tests	.28	.31	.46
Grades and attitudes in psychology course	.48	.56	.62
Business failures using financial ratios	.50	.53	.67
Students' ratings of teaching effectiveness	.35	.56	.91
Performance of life insurance salesmen	.13	.14	.43
IQ scores using Rorschach tests	.47	.51	.54
Mean (across all studies)	**.33**	**.39**	**.64**

- financial reporting
- regulatory compliance
- key business decisions such as pricing, credit risk, supplier management
- legal obligations
- intellectual property/competitive advantage

is deemed "critical data" and should be managed closely with all the practices you will learn in this book.

If the objectives are specific and measurable, the data manager's job is easier. For example, if the marketing department's goal is to attract 1,000 new customers over the next calendar year, then the data manager can clearly begin to identify the data needed to help marketing. First, she defines "new" customer and then looks for ways in the company's systems to identify this entity. If the objectives of the business are not specific and measurable, the data manager's job is more difficult.

With objectives clearly articulated, also consider what else is needed to meet the business requirement fully. Take for example a company that uses customer satisfaction as a way to reward sales representatives and compute bonuses. If the company lacks an unbiased system for collecting and managing customer responses to satisfaction surveys, then the data collected may not meet the objectives. Business processes need to align to the objectives as well. Without changing the business process, the data will become the scapegoat because it is the most visible to management—the outcome of bad process.

Basic Data Characteristics and Attributes

Measuring any business objective or providing insight to business managers requires data that has some basic characteristics and attributes. For example:

- **Data should be accurate**. That simply means that it should reflect reality consistently and over time. Often measuring the accuracy of data is difficult because accuracy requires that you have a standard to measure against. Take for example the accuracy of a company name such as Kraft. How do you decide that Kraft is the name of the company? Do you rely on the legal name of this company from government registries or chamber of commerce listings? Do you rely on your sales representative to acquire the correct name from his buyer? In this case as in most cases of data accuracy, the question becomes which process is considered the most reliable in providing the most accurate data, not which data is most accurate.

- **Data should be timely.** Timely means that it reflects the most recent reality and is available when needed by the business. Business changes constantly. The data that you received yesterday about sales in China will be different than the data you get today. Some businesses require that they have up-to-the-minute information about customer transactions. Online retailers are one example. Manufacturing and warehousing operations often require data that is accurate to the minute. For example, a General Motor assembly line could lose millions of dollars if parts are not available when they are needed. Many see this need for data to be timely as a system issue, but again the data carried by the system is the result of business processes that create and update data to ensure its currency.

- **Data should be reliable.** If the data you received yesterday about the sales in China showed that you should increase your inventories because of an increase in opportunities in that country, you wouldn't feel comfortable about the data if today it showed an exactly opposite situation. Again, the data is all that a manufacturing manager might see as he readies the inventories for shipment. But the root cause of unreliable data is process first and then systems.

- **Data should be easily attainable when you need it.** Here again, the business manager relies on the systems to deliver data to her. The data should be accessible, easy to understand and meaningful to the manager that uses it for decision-making. In the next section, you'll see how the data can be presented, but now the business requirement is that the data that is collected be readily and easily available. Delivering data to the business user can be accomplished in a myriad of ways, from reports to online applications. Ensuring that it reaches the right decision-maker at the appropriate time is also something that the data systems must consider.

- **Data should be capable of being manipulated easily and rapidly.** Business decisions don't usually just arrive, delivered with a bow through the systems that your company deploys. Decisions often require inputs (data) from a variety of systems and functions, and often from both providers internal to your company and external as well. To make data-based decisions requires that data not only be easily accessible, but also easily accumulated and manipulated. Tools that allow data to be brought together from various functions and manipulated abound on the market today. The most notable is SAS, but other tools allow for this type of integration. If you require certain types of data to be integrated constantly such as revenue transactions with customer data, then you could build these relationships into your data warehouse and use tools such as Business Objects or Siebel Analytics to gain quick, easy access to the information you need for decision-making.

  In the world of Web analytics, data must not only be easily accessible, but it must also often be available immediately for use in sophisticated predictive models. For example, sites such as Amazon, Netflix and countless other e-tailers use the information about what books you buy, or what movies you rent, to present to you options for other books and movies that you might like. These models are based both on business rules and advanced statistical models that can predict what might be of interest to you. This requires systems that can easily and rapidly manage information that flows from a customer's actions on the Web site. If the data lacks integrity or is inconsistent in any way, the models fail to provide the customer with the experience that leads to greater interaction on the site and larger purchases. Here data plays a very important role in achieving the business goals.

A companywide data management program will ensure the basic characteristics and attributes of data will be met in a consistent, most economical way. Subsequent chapters will detail how to implement this type of program.

Creating Effective Data

Simply put, creating effective data consists of:

- First aligning data management to business objectives.
- Designing business processes with good data management in mind.
- Creating trusted, high-quality data structures that are shareable.
- Architecting systems for good data management.
- Using common tools and technology for data management.
- Ensuring an ongoing data quality program.
- Monitoring data metrics.

The process for generating effective data is outlined in Exhibit 1.2.

Exhibit 1.2. Steps in Creating Effective Data

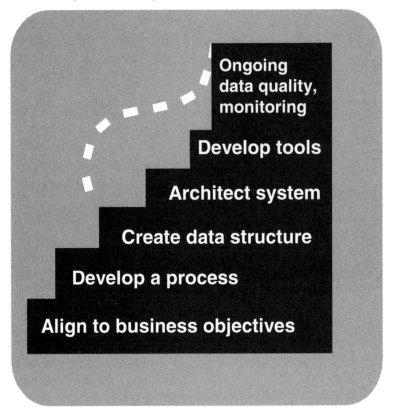

How Do You Know to Trust the Data?

The executive on the aisle seat in the 767 headed to Chicago has just grabbed a sales report from his briefcase. He occupies the time during takeoff by perusing the list of figures from each of his sales teams. Sally in Omaha looks like she's well on her way to making her quota in the first three weeks of the quarter. Joe, however, is struggling. This executive trusts the data that he sees on the page until he gets to the figure for Anthony. Here the numbers make no sense. Anthony has been a solid performer for the three years he's been on the team. He consistently makes or exceeds his quota. If the executive has any challenge with Anthony it is that he makes his quota always at the last minute of the last week in the quarter. The report he holds in his hand, however, shows Anthony having already achieved his quota for this quarter—three weeks into the quarter. Suddenly, the executive is worried. Not about Anthony and his performance, but about the data.

The tendency to doubt the numbers or the data may be the first reaction of your executive team. If it is, here are some ways to help your executives learn to trust the numbers that they see. All of these actions build on one another and are valuable in helping to establish data management as a discipline within your company if you seek ways to integrate them into the company's management systems. That means make this a practice at your monthly or quarterly reviews. Demonstrate this behavior by putting it into practice with the data teams as well as the other business groups that the data team serves.

When evaluating data in reports, use this checklist:

- **Compare it to your "gut."** Although we've been arguing that your gut is not smarter than your head, here's a place where you need to put the gut into action. As noted in the example above, the sales executive didn't quite understand why Anthony had broken with his usual performance for this quarter. This kind of "gut check" helps to identify places to begin investigating data. Undoubtedly, this sales exec will call his business analyst who provided the report as soon as his flight lands.

- **Ask questions, listen carefully to the answers.** The sales exec with the challenge to understand Anthony's performance will first ask questions of the report he holds. The business analyst will be able to tell him what the data says and if there are any issues with the way it was collected or reported. The sales executive would be wise to ask questions about how the data was collected, what made this period different from others, if there were any system changes or updates that would have affected the data. Asking questions helps both the executive and the data manager to better understand how the data reflects the business. What the sales exec may find is that Anthony's sudden quota achievement is the result of one customer who needed to purchase early because of a compliance project that the company has initiated.

- **Refer to trends, not absolutes.** Just as the sales exec zeroed in on Anthony's performance for the quarter by noticing the difference in the normal route to quota achievement, most managers prefer to evaluate the trends in data over the absolutes. For example, Anthony's total achievement was not what signaled the sales exec, but instead the percentage of achievement this quarter as compared to past quarters. Even if the data in your systems is suspect, if it is collected, managed and reported on consistently, the trends reflected are as, or more, important than the absolutes reflected by the data.

- **Test one system against another.** When he reaches his business analyst, the sales exec may ask that the data he sees in the report be verified through another source. This is a great way to make sure that your data accurately reflects reality. Each report generated from core data sources should have a way to validate its results. For example, generating a sales report from the sales opportunity data should be compared to and validated by the order entry systems. Because each systems output becomes the input for another system, evaluating how the data is managed across these junctures often helps to identify any issues that you might have with the data itself.

- **Look for correlations; don't expect causality.** Executives from every faction of the business are fond of the "why" question. For example, why did Anthony make his number so fast this quarter? Although data in the sales system may answer that question, it may also lead to more questions. Most executives expect that the answer to *why* can or should be derived from data. That's possible most of the time, but not always. Often the data presents the situation as it is. Background, root cause or any other enlightening context to the numbers is not always immediately visible. Data mining and business intelligence modeling can help highlight phenomena in the business, but can't always prove that one event or data point caused another to happen. For example, just because sales have gone up in eastern Illinois and coincidentally you've also hired two new business partners in that area, doesn't necessarily mean that these two partners are responsible for the increase in sales. These two facts may be correlated, but there is also no proof that one caused the other.

- **Develop a companywide data management program.** Whether your company is one person or 100,000, your data is the lifeblood of that enterprise. Companywide data management programs touch all aspects of your business and make everyone aware of the value of data. Remember when Ford Motor Company realized that it was being outsold by the Japanese auto makers because of the poor quality of their cars? The program Ford put in place became their advertising slogan: *At Ford, Quality is Job 1.* Like Ford, data and its quality need to be Job 1 at your company.

Summary

Trusting the data that appears in your reports or your executive information system begins with active involvement by business leaders. Business involvement in the data selection, creation and collection will ensure the critical data to run the business meets the business need. Understanding that data, asking questions about what it means and listening carefully to the answers ensures the data can be trusted. Using data to help make business decisions is as much art as science. You need to know when to rely on the data and how much to rely on it. One hundred percent data quality is not practical or achievable. While most business decisions are better when based on solid, accurate data, there will always be the requirement to make judgment calls. Making them with data simply improves your chances of being right.

2

Data: The Key to a Complete View of Your Customer

As Stephen Covey says in *The 7 Habits of Highly Effective People*, begin with the end in mind. This directive works wonders in the data world, especially when you are looking to use data for key business decisions. Starting from the end in data terms means starting with the report that you want to derive from the data. The data that you require for reporting is structured data that can be easily aggregated to give you a view of your business at a particular point in time. In fact the very definition of report—*an account or statement describing in detail an event, situation, or the like, usually as the result of observation, inquiry, etc*—suggests that the information reflects a particular point in time or span of time.

Data and the 360-Degree View

Reports, as we know them, consist of data arranged in ways so as to help us understand better the business processes that are measured. These reports can tell us how we did financially, monitor a process, or even provide customer insight. The 360-degree view of the customer is the one report or data view that has generated a lot of interest from managers over the past few years. As large enterprises begin to gather their data into large enterprise data warehouses, data from throughout the organization is brought together. Suddenly, the shipping data can relate to the sales opportunity data and all of that can relate to the customer service records.

But the 360-degree view of the customer goes beyond just gathering the data into one physical location; it's a strategy that enables virtual assembly of all customer information at the point where and when you need that information to better serve the customer. For example, if your customer service department must provide upgrades to your product line, the information about which customers have your old products is key to delivering value to the customer. Shipping the new product to the right address is important as well, but understanding also whether the customer is satisfied with the existing product may alter your approach. What companies have found in providing this 360-degree view is that merely cleaning up their

Exhibit 2.1. Benefits of the 360-Degree View

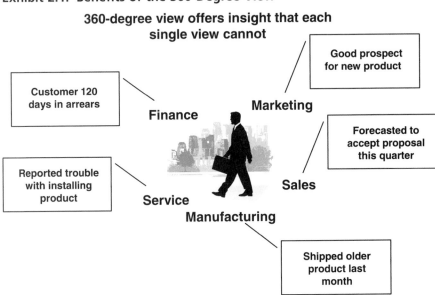

360-degree view offers insight that each single view cannot

Good prospect for new product

Customer 120 days in arrears

Finance

Marketing

Forecasted to accept proposal this quarter

Reported trouble with installing product

Service

Sales

Manufacturing

Shipped older product last month

data in spots or departments is no longer sufficient. They need to clean up all data that affects each customer and then make sure that each data set integrates well with others. This one requirement has driven more companies to create a customer data management program than any other.

In the drive to a 360-degree view, your executives may be the most skeptical. Explaining why you need complete, accurate data is not always obvious to them. Being able to produce this view of the customer helps them understand. As Scott Gidley, cofounder and chief technology officer for DataFlux, said: "If you tell [C-level execs] '50% of the data in this one particular column is null,' they're not going to get it. But if you tell them, 'Because of the way we're set up now, we can't send invoices to our major accounts with manual intervention,' they start to pay attention."[1] Relating data quality, availability and accessibility to business issues is often the best way to make the case for initiatives that help drive quality data.

Like a full-length mirror shows your entire body—flaws and all—this view of your customer should show how your customer interacts with your business. It will show the reality of how the customer sees the company front to back—good or bad. This view is widely considered the foundation for providing a unique customer experience with your company and its products. Although it is not an easy view to derive usually from the data as it is initially stored in a company, it can be the most

---

[1] "A true view of the customer requires data 'symbiosis'" by Larry Dobrow (Peppers & Rogers Group), SearchCRM.com, January 2, 2007.

important single driver to overall company revenue growth and customer loyalty growth.

The 360-degree view includes data from any process you operate within the company as well as any external information you might have on the customer derived from other third-party data sources. In other words, a complete view of your customers includes not only what you know about them, but also what is known about them outside of the company. Internally, contracts, business relationships stored in CRM systems, sales transaction history, installed inventory, customer satisfaction, Web registration information, recent service-oriented events, customer visits by sales and executives, and opportunities all generate a part of the view. Externally, data on your customers can be as global as a D&B number or as specific as information on your competitor's installations within your customer accounts. The definition of what constitutes a complete 360-degree view varies by process within your company.

Obstacles to a 360-Degree View

What makes *this* data project so difficult? Here's a quick list of the barriers to a 360-degree view:

1. **Lots of data sources.** Each source has to be clearly understood, modeled and evaluated for its contribution to the view. Data quality must be evaluated as well and quality standards fixed to ensure that contributions to the view are accurate.

2. **No clear business owner for customer data.** The majority of business processes within a company support the "customer." Therefore, getting consensus on the business rules and solving the business issues that come up during a project designed to provide a 360-degree view take time. Conflicting business requirements may also require a "mediator" to make a final decision. Here's where a senior-level executive who is also a data evangelist can help.

3. **Matching customer records from multiple sources is an art form, not a predictable science.** When you bring all the data on all of your customers into one location, whether physical or virtual, you have to be able to match a customer record in one system with a customer record in another. The completeness of the data, the accuracy and integrity of the data, may make matching record to record a very difficult job. Couple with that the fact that matching is more art than science, and you have a challenge. Matching is an iterative process that requires good business rules, enabled technology and data experts. If there is an Achilles' heel to any data project, it is this one. Investing in good matching tools or securing a firm that specializes in matching data are both good options to support this effort.

4. **Project rate and pace.** Because of points 1 and 2 above, completing the 360-view of a customer is a multi-year project that has to be approached in phases. A recent Harvard Business Review article studied two customer data projects: Harris and United Airlines. The average time for both projects was four to six years. So, tackling a customer data project is a long-term endeavor.

   Here are some ways to manage this challenge. Identify the most important function within your business that gives you today the best view of your customer and begin there. For example, if your sales organization is disciplined about how it collects and manages data, start with the sales view. If, like most companies, your best view of the customer is in the shipping department, start there. Wherever your starting point, make sure that you communicate that this is just the beginning and that you will be tackling all functions where a view of the customer is possible. Articulate early and often the order in which you are building this view—sales, order entry, shipping, marketing, etc.

5. **Large multi-year projects require company commitment to "stay the course."** Many companies don't have the fortitude for multi-year projects and reduce the financial budget for these projects year after year. You may find that providing a 360-degree view of the customer falls into this "multi-year" program. The solution to keeping focus and funding for a long-range plan of this magnitude is to provide progress on a quarterly basis. Again, articulating where you are headed and showing progress on a quarterly basis is the secret to making this journey successful.

6. **Inconsistencies in the definition of customer fields across applications.** No single word in business is more misunderstood from the data perspective than "customer." Ask any department within your company what the definition of a customer is and you will undoubtedly end up with several definitions—each appropriate for that department's function. When trying to create a 360-degree view, having a consistent definition is a *must*. Getting to that definition requires compromise, collaboration and a clear vision of why it is important to arrive at a standard definition. If you've developed a strong master data management strategy and assembled a quality team, this project can be a crowning accomplishment.

7. **"360-degree view" means different things to different parts of the organization and will continue to change once your systems to support it have been deployed.** The project to provide a 360-degree view of the customer won't be considered complete until all the stakeholders believe their view is complete. If you start with sales and provide a view of the customer for the sales force, you've only started. The view for customer service, shipping and mar-

keting must also be complete; otherwise the organization may see the project as a failure. Your other challenge is this view may change as the business evolves. For example, when you begin your project with the sales department, you may have only been interested in supporting face-to-face salespeople with customer information. As your business grows, however, you may find that providing customer information online is just as important. Now the view of the customer for sales must also include an online view. Staying flexible and ready to incorporate all changes into the view is your key to success.

8. **Customer data is perishable and it perishes rapidly at the rate of 30% to 40% a year.** Not only must you manage change within your organization such as systems, new business challenges and reorganizations, but you must manage the inevitable decay of the data itself. And you need to manage this even while you are attempting to pull together systems, organizations and processes that provide a 360-degree view. No organization in business today feels more like a juggler in a circus act than does the data manager assigned to create a 360-degree customer view. You're in the center ring with three balls in the air, standing on one foot and balancing a bowling pin on the other. Get the feeling?

Providing a 360-degree view of the customer can be the most challenging data exercise your company can undertake. The benefits are great if used to better serve the customer. The challenges are many. In the end, your biggest decision is whether this view will add value to customer and hence the shareholders.

3

Data and Compliance

Financial deceit cases like Enron and WorldCom coupled with identity theft like T J Maxx, have put pressure on companies to protect consumers and shareholders from these types of corporate theft. In the aftermath of these scandals, regulatory bodies have introduced legislation to protect us. Companies of all types and sizes, public and private, not-for-profit and educational groups, have all been affected. Legislation is raising the awareness of executives for the need to step up their compliance posture.

> Regulatory compliance not only means watching out for your company's financial reporting with tougher, more transparent accounting practices, but it also means managing the collection, access, exchange, classification, and storage of your company's data against standards.

While the United States has been leading the regulatory compliance on financial reporting and transparency, Europe has led the way on personal privacy. Other countries are rapidly following and adopting much of the same legislation. Surprisingly, emerging nations, such as China, may be slow to address privacy, but when they do their rules are often stricter than those of Europe or the US.

The impact of noncompliance can be very serious as the Enron example demonstrated. Besides the obvious financial consequences, there are legal and reputation costs to your business (see Exhibit 3.1), such as the loss of credibility with your employees, stockholders and customers.

Most laws do not distinguish between intent and inadvertent violations. Neither does the court of public opinion. Noncompliance issues are big news and scandals are often fodder for the daily news teams.

Managing compliance in today's regulatory environment requires good processes, good policies, good systems, good documentation AND good data. Regulatory and governmental bodies require companies to provide data and documents in a variety of compliance reports along with annual assessments that verify the processes associated with customers, orders and products are properly managed.

Exhibit 3.1. Cost of Noncompliance

Legal	Financial	Reputation
• Civil stockholder lawsuits	• Liquidity problems through loss of funds	• Loss of credibility with employees, customers and stockholders
• Senior management incarceration	• Increased cost of capital	• Delisting of company stock by SEC
• Investigative + legal time and cost	• Fines, penalties	
	• Bankruptcy	

Attesting to proper management includes the appropriate accountability and transparency supported by metrics and documentation.

All these realities are forcing requirements on the data to be more accurate, more timely, more integrated and with higher levels of documentation and controls. The technical data architectures of the systems that produce the data are being taxed, as many of these legacy systems were not designed for this level of data quality and timely processing. Business managers and data managers are being forced to monitor high volumes of data in real time at a time when companies are pressed to do more with less.

While health and retail companies face intense scrutiny because of their vast amounts of consumer data, business-to-business (B2B) companies are not immune from compliance and privacy laws. However, those doing business with other businesses often feel they are immune—after all, they don't have to worry about consumer identity theft, right? Wrong. In reality, B2B firms are just as susceptible to faulty or fraudulent information as consumer firms, if not more. There are more data handoffs from the actual customer transactions to the B2B process, introducing opportunity for data quality defects and fraud by a third party. B2B firms are also not immune to the financial reporting regulations.

Both consumer and B2B companies have the additional problem of managing and storing huge volumes of emails and files in order to remain compliant with current laws and regulations. Whether the requirement to maintain this information is three months or fifty years, this puts an additional pressure on the data management team not only from a systems perspective (Just how much hard drive space do you need?), but also from a process perspective (Do you need nightly backups? For how long do we archive data?) Employees now have access to huge amounts of data from the Web. With the growth in messaging, it is estimated that 1,000 users generate 1,000,000,000,000 MBs or 1TB of data annually. With 99.999% uptime and 7 × 24-hour operation, corporations need to evaluate their current way of managing data. Data access, flexibility and timeliness come at a cost of higher data risk. Today almost 70% of email generated by organizations has legal or compliance significance.

In part, it was TJX Corporation's haphazard data management practices that caused one of North America's largest data breaches when millions of personal records were hacked outside a few T J Maxx stores in Florida. The company admitted to keeping too much personal data on their customers for too long without proper security.

So whether you are in a consumer company or a B2B company, compliance is here to stay. Understanding all the regulatory requirements that impact your company and the industry in which you operate is a critical step to devising a holistic, proactive approach to compliance. Addressing each regulation in a piecemeal fashion is inefficient, costly and can drive your business and data teams crazy.

Compliance and Data Management

Fortunately for you, the data challenges posed by the compliance and legislative standards are not unlike other data challenges in your company. Having high quality, up-to-date, integrated business data for financial reporting and coupling that with the proper security, privacy and risk management processes are all required to run an effective, profitable company in today's wired and wireless environments.

> **Regulatory compliance is the 2nd most cited reason for adopting a data quality program.**
>
> *Gartner Group, Nov. 2005*

Regulation has become a key driver for implementing an effective data management and data quality program. In a November 2005 study on data quality, the Gartner Group analyst reported that supporting regulatory compliance efforts was the second most cited reason for adopting a data quality program. (For the curious, the number one reason cited for adopting a data quality program was to increase the user adoption of a major application.) If this is the case for your company, take comfort in that the data disciplines required for compliance can and should be leveraged to improve data management and data quality for other business processes. Implementing the data management practices discussed in this book provides the solid foundation for managing compliance and legislative standards imposed by information security, information privacy and financial reporting.

Let's discuss each of the compliance topics in more detail with its corresponding data management implications. In all three cases, the data management implications are very similar. The companywide data management program will address the following aspects of the overall compliance programs:

- How should the data be classified?
- Where is the data?
- Where and what documentation is required about the data?
- Who is the owner?
- Who should have access to the data?
- What are the possible data issues and risks?
- What testing and controls need to be put in place?
- What data standards should be developed
- How should compliance be measured and tracked?

CAUTION: Heed this word of caution as you begin to collect all the regulations and standards that affect your industry. Compliance details are sketchy and implementation details will not be spelled out. Regulations and standards are meant to be applied to companies of all shapes and sizes, hence they are written in a general tone by intent. Also, what constitutes "protected data" varies by jurisdiction. Laws are set at the national, state and municipal level and laws are changing. Your organizations must keep a close eye on the changing legislation and be proactive with a corporate response to new legislation. In most companies, the finance, legal and compliance departments are the most up to date with the regulations that will affect the firm. These departments must use sound business judgment to determine how to apply these standards and regulations in the company. Establishing a separate information security organization and/or a chief privacy officer are other ways corporations drive accountability and implementation responsibility.

Many consulting companies specialize in helping companies through this evaluation phase. We provide some guidance on the data management implications of adopting these standards to get you started.

Information Security Compliance

Information security compliance means properly protecting the information resources of the firm with the appropriate accountability, risk management, security measures and controls commensurate with the value of the information. Information resources can be in any form: electronic, paper or intangible (speech or conversation). Electronic form includes databases as well as unstructured data in emails, soft copy documents, spreadsheets and Web information. Information security addresses three factors often referred to as the CIA triad:

1. confidentiality
2. integrity
3. availability

Confidentiality. Information must only be accessed, used, copied, or disclosed by persons who have been authorized to access, use, copy, or disclose the information, and then only when there is a genuine need to access, use, copy or disclose the information. A breach of confidentiality occurs when confidential information has been, or may have been, accessed, used, copied, or disclosed to, or by, someone who was not authorized to have access to the information.

Confidentiality applies to all kinds of data. Making a customer list available to a third party may constitute a violation of confidentiality, especially if the customer list is comprised of customers of another of your distributors or business partners. Confidentiality always applies to highly sensitive financial data. In most publicly traded companies there are rules about who has access to current financial information. One solid rule to apply with confidential information is "when in doubt, don't let it out."

A common challenge here is determining levels of confidentiality, such as "internal use" versus "highly confidential." Select terminology that is easily understood and actionable so that employees will not be confused.

Integrity. Information integrity means that data is accurate, complete and cannot be created, changed, or deleted without authorization. Loss of integrity occurs when an employee accidentally, or with malicious intent, deletes important data files. A loss of integrity can occur if a computer virus is released onto the computer. A loss of integrity can occur when an employee changes the price of a product without authorization. Managing who and how to access information is critical to ensure integrity is maintained.

Availability. Data availability means that the computing systems and security controls used to process information are available and functioning correctly when needed.

Information Security and Risk Management

Discussing information security without risk management is impossible. The 2006 CISA (Certified Information Security Auditor) Review Manual defines risk management as "the process of identifying vulnerabilities and threats to the information resources used by an organization in achieving business objectives, and deciding what countermeasures, if any, to take in reducing risk to an acceptable level, based on the value of the information resource to the organization." Simply said, assessing risk and its impact on your company is the basis by which information security is addressed and planned. Risk is the likelihood that something bad will happen to an informational asset. Vulnerability is a weakness that can cause harm to an informational asset. A threat is anything (man-made or act of nature) that has the potential to cause harm.

The likelihood that a threat will use a vulnerability to cause harm creates a risk. When a threat does use a vulnerability to inflict harm, it has an impact. In the context of information security, the impact can be a loss of availability, integrity, and confidentiality, and possibly subsequent losses such as the loss of life or of real property. Identifying and eliminating all risks in the firm is not the goal. Vigilance in managing risk is. Risks associated with information security are managed by implementing proper physical, logical and administrative controls commensurate with the information's value. Those risks that cannot be identified effectively or eliminated are called residual risks. Even these risks, however, are minimized by vigilance and consistent management.

Information Security Legislation and Standards

Following is a list of current legislation and standards that affect information security:

Exhibit 3.2. Compliance Laws and Standards

Compliance	Laws and Standards
Information Security	COBIT (Control Objective for Information & Related Technology)
	FFIEC (Federal Finance Institution Examination Council)
	Information Security Forum Standards of good practice
	ISO/IEC 17799
	Basel Standards
Data Privacy	CAN-SPAM (Controlling the Assault of Non-Solicited Pornography and Marketing Act)
	HIPAA (Health Insurance Portability, Accountability Act)
	COPPA (Children's Online Privacy Protection Act)
	EUDPD (European Union Data Protection Directive)
	Safe Harbor
	PCI (Payment Card Industry Data Security Standard)
	Japan's Personal Information Protection Act
	Gramm-Leach Bliley Act
	USA Patriot Act
	SB 1386 California Civil Code
Financial Reporting	Sarbanes Oxley Act
	COSO (Committee or Sponsoring Organization of Treadway Commission)

COBIT (Control Objectives for Information and Related Technology) is a set of best practice processes, measures and indicators issued by the IT Governance Institute. COBIT is a generally accepted standard, both domestically and internationally, for good IT security, governance and control practices. The COBIT framework defines 34 high-level control objectives. COBIT is used by auditors, IT users, IT managers, business managers and process owners.

FFIEC (Federal Finance Institution Examination Council) is a formal interagency body empowered to prescribe uniform principles, standards, and report forms for the federal examination of financial institutions. The council can also make recommendations to promote uniformity in the supervision of financial institutions. Guidelines include enforcement options for financial institutions that do not establish adequate information security programs.

Information Security Forum Standard of Good Practice was produced by the Information Security Forum, an international association of over 270 organizations that fund research and development in information security. This standard of good practice addresses five primary aspects of information security:

- security management
- system development
- critical business applications
- computer installations
- networks

The Information Security Forum also provides the Information Security Status Survey, an assessment tool that allows companies to make a quantitative and comprehensive assessment of how well they conform to the Standard of Good Practice.

ISO/IEC 17799 is a code of practice for information security management. It recommends that the following be examined during a risk assessment:

- security policy
- organization of information security
- asset management
- human resources security
- physical and environmental security, communications and operations management
- access control
- information systems acquisition
- development and maintenance
- information security incident management
- business continuity management
- regulatory compliance

BASEL Standards. BASEL I and BASEL II are international banking standards developed by the BASEL Committee on Banking Supervision. This is an informal forum of senior banking authorities from the G-10 countries who encourage common policies and standards. The regulatory standards address how much capital that banks have to set aside and how to quantify and manage risk. The greater the risk exposure for the bank, the greater the amount of capital the bank needs to hold to ensure its stability.

BASEL Risk Management Principles for Electronic Banking is a reference guide developed by the Bank of International Settlement (BIS). BIS is an international organization that fosters cooperation among central banks in pursuit of financial and monetary stability. The BASEL Committee on Banking Supervision usually meets at the BIS. The reference guide provides best practices in security and risk management for e-banking. The BIS believes e-banking poses additional security risks that need to be managed more closely than traditional banking.

Information Security and Data Management Implications

Proper classification of the business value, sensitivity and criticality of information is critical to establishing proper information security controls. The data management program should address the following aspects of the information security compliance program:

- What data should be classified as public, sensitive, private, and confidential?
- What is the business value of this data? What is the impact if this data is not available?
- Where is this data? Who is the owner?
- What documentation about the data is required? Where should it be kept?
- What breaches are possible? What is the risk of the breach?
- What controls need to developed to manage the risks?
- Who should have access?
- What compliance metric tracking is necessary?
- What data standards should be developed to ensure confidentiality, integrity and availability?
- How should specific sensitive information such as email permissions or credit card information be managed?

Data Privacy Compliance means properly protecting the collecting, processing, storing and dissemination of sensitive personal information that may lead to identity theft or improper disclosure of private data. The following information is most affected by data privacy issues:

- Health information
- Criminal justice information
- Financial information
- Genetic information
- Location information

Data Privacy Legislation and Standards

The right to data privacy is much more heavily regulated in Europe than in the United States and Canada, and is becoming more of a business consideration in emerging countries such as China and India. Here is a sample of all the different data privacy laws, legislation and standards that govern the use of data today:

The CAN-SPAM Act of 2003 (Controlling the Assault of Non-Solicited Pornography and Marketing Act) governs commercial email and establishes penalties for spammers and companies who promote their products through spam. The law primarily concerns email that markets a product or service; it excludes email sent in the course of a transaction. The Federal Trade Commission (FTC) enforces the law, which bans false or misleading header information, prohibits deceptive subject lines, and requires that email give recipients a way to opt-out of further communications. A violation of the CAN-SPAM Act can carry a fine up to $11,000.

Health Insurance Portability and Accountability Act (HIPAA) is also known as the Kennedy–Kassenbaum Act. This act requires the United States Department of Health and Human Services (HHS) to establish national standards for electronic health care transactions and national identifiers for providers, health plans, and employers. It also addresses the security and privacy of health data. As the industry adopts these standards for efficiency and effectiveness, the nation's health care system will improve its use of electronic data interchange.

Children's Online Privacy Protection Act of 1998 (COPPA) is a US federal law enforced by the Federal Trade Commission that protects the online collection of the personal information from children under 13 years of age. The act applies to Web site operators and online service providers. It specifies when and how a parent or guardian's consent is acquired and it restricts marketing to children under age 13.

European Union Data Protection Directive (EUDPD—1995) standardizes the protection of data privacy for citizens throughout the European Union (EU) by providing baseline requirements that all member states must achieve through implementing national legislation. This directive is primarily responsible for ensuring the privacy of personal data—its acquisition, use and retention.

Safe Harbor is a framework created by the US Department of Commerce to comply with the European Union directive on data protection. The Federal Trade Commission oversees Safe Harbor. Because the European directive introduced a legal risk to organizations that transfer the personal data of European citizens to servers in America, the US implemented this

Safe Harbor program. It ensures that US organizations avoid the penalty they could face under EU law if the privacy protection of the US was found to be weaker than that of the EU. Under the program, the European Commission agreed to forbid European citizens from suing US companies certified as a Safe Harbor for transmitting personal data into the US.

US companies can participate in the Safe Harbor program if they provide:

- **Notice**—Inform individuals that their data is being collected and ensure that they know how it will be used.
- **Choice**—Provide individuals with a way to opt out on the collection of personal data and to forbid the transfer of the data to third parties.
- **Onward Transfer**—Transfer of data to third parties may only occur if the third party organization follows adequate data protection principles.
- **Security**—Reasonable efforts are made to prevent loss of collected information.
- **Data Integrity**—Data must be relevant and reliable for the purpose for which it was collected.
- **Access**—Provide individuals with access to information held about them, and correct or delete it if it is inaccurate or upon request from the individual.
- **Enforcement**—There must be effective means of enforcing these rules.

Payment Card Industry Data Security Standard protects the use of credit card information. The four major credit card associations in the United States (Visa, MasterCard, American Express, and Discover Network) adopted this consolidated data security standard. Merchants who accept these cards must comply with the following requirements:

Build and Maintain a Secure Network
- Install and maintain a firewall configuration to protect cardholder data.
- Do not use vendor-supplied defaults for system passwords and other security parameters

Protect Cardholder Data
- Protect stored cardholder data.
- Encrypt transmission of cardholder data across open, public networks.

Maintain a Vulnerability Management Program
- Use and regularly update anti-virus software.
- Develop and maintain secure systems and applications.

Implement Strong Access Control Measures
- Restrict access to cardholder data by business on a need-to-know basis.
- Assign a unique ID to each person with computer access.
- Restrict physical access to cardholder data.

Regularly Monitor and Test Networks
- Track and monitor all access to network resources and cardholder data.
- Regularly test security systems and processes.

Maintain an Information Security Policy
- Maintain a policy that addresses information security.

Japan's Personal Information Protection Act (2005) is Japan's policy for protecting personal information. It applies to government or private entities that collect, handle, or use the personal information of 5,000 or more individuals. The act protects individuals by regulating the handling of information by private sector businesses. However, it only protects individuals and does not apply to corporations or associations.

Gramm–Leach Bliley Act (GLBA), also known as the Financial Moderation Act of 1999, protects personal information held by financial institutions. Financial institutions are defined as all companies that offer financial products such as loans, financial and investment advice or insurance. GLBA has three components:

1. The Financial Privacy Rule governs the collection and disclosure of customer personal financial information by financial companies *and* companies that receive the information, even if not a financial institution.
2. The Safeguard Rule requires financial companies to have a security plan to protect the confidentiality and integrity of their customers. This rule also applies to companies that collect personal financial information such as a credit company. The Safeguard rule is enforced by the Federal Trade Commission.
3. Pre-texting protects consumers from individuals and companies that obtain their financial information under false pretenses.

GLBA gives authority to eight federal agencies and the states to administer and enforce the Financial Privacy Rule and the Safeguard Rule. These two regulations apply to "financial institutions," which include not only banks, securities firms, and insurance companies, but also companies providing many other types of financial products and services to consumers. Among these services are lending, brokering or servicing any type of consumer loan, transferring or safeguarding money, preparing individual tax returns, providing financial advice or credit counseling, providing residential real estate settlement services, collecting consumer debts and an array of other activities. Such non-traditional "financial institutions" are regulated by the FTC.

Similar, but more restrictive, laws have been established in many states and municipalities. Firms operating in those jurisdictions or who have customers or employees living in those jurisdictions are required to comply with those laws. It has been especially challenging for firms to comply with diverse, sometimes conflicting requirements.

USA Patriot Act, also called Uniting and Strengthening by Providing Appropriate Tools Required to Intercept and Obstruct Terrorism Act of 2001, was passed after Sept 11, 2001. This act gives US law enforcement agencies expanded authority to search telephone and email communication, medical and financial records and other records without the individuals' permission or a court order. It was enacted to fight against domestic and international terrorism. Under the Patriot Act, companies must cooperate with US law enforcement to provide this information. The Patriot Act has been criticized for weakening privacy and civil liberties.

SB 1386-California Civil Code requires companies doing business in California or having California resident information to disclose any security breaches of unencrypted personal information. This code was the first law of its kind in the United States.

In February 2005, Choice Point, a corporation that collects and compiles information that includes personal and financial information on millions of consumers, disclosed that it had been the victim of a security breach that had resulted in the sale to a criminal enterprise of personal information from almost 145,000 people. California's bill made it necessary for Choice Point to report this breach. Thirty-five states have enacted legislation requiring companies to disclose security breaches involving personal information.

Data Privacy and Data Management Implications

The data management program should address the following aspects of the data privacy compliance program.

- What specific data attributes make up personal or sensitive information?
- Where is all the data that contains these attributes?
- Who owns the data?
- What controls should be developed?
- How do we ensure the data is correct?
- What breaches are possible? What are the risks to the breach?
- What compliance tracking metrics are necessary?
- What data standards need to be developed to ensure data privacy?

Financial Reporting Legislation and Standards

Financial reporting compliance ensures the transparency, proper controls and reliability of financial data to investors. Here are a few of the financial laws, regulations and standards that apply to data:

The **Sarbanes-Oxley Act** was passed in the US in response to the Enron and WorldCom financial reporting scandals. SOX, as it has come to be known, was enacted into law in 2002 to protect investors by improving the accuracy and reliability of company disclosures. The act covers all companies that are governed by the Securities and Exchange Commission. Sarbanes-Oxley outlines requirements for board membership, board responsibility, public accounting firm responsibility and company staff responsibility. There are several key provisions:

- **Oversight.** Creation of the Public Company Accounting Oversight Board (PCAOB) to oversee auditors of public corporations.

- **Auditor Accountability.** Public companies must evaluate and disclose the effectiveness of their internal controls as they relate to financial reporting (Section 404). Independent auditors must "attest" (i.e., agree or qualify) to such disclosures.

- **Corporate Responsibility and Penalty.** Chief Executive officers and Chief Financial officers are to certify the accuracy and completeness of their financial reporting (Section 302) and effectiveness of internal controls (Section 404). The act also provides for significantly longer maximum jail sentences and larger fines for corporate executives who knowingly and willfully misstate financial statements and violate securities law.

- **Enhanced Financial Disclosures.** The reporting requirements for financial transactions and stock transactions of corporate officers are enhanced. They require timely reporting of material changes in financial condition and specific enhanced reviews by the SEC or its agents of corporate reports.

- **Enhanced auditing requirements:**
  —Auditor must be independent. The act specifically includes outright bans on certain types of work for audit clients and pre-certification by the company's audit committee on all other non-audit work.
  —Public companies must have fully independent audit committees that oversee the relationship between the company and its auditor.

- **Additional disclosure.** All communication must be archived and transparent. Auditable systems must be created for recording transactions and business correspondence. Accelerated reporting of insider trading.

- **Protection.** Whistle-blower protection for employee who disclose corporate fraud.

Committee of Sponsoring Organizations (COSO) of the Treadway Commission is a private-sector initiative funded by five major accounting institutions: the American Institute of Certified Public Accountants, the American Accounting Association, the Financial Executive Institute, the Institute of Internal Auditors and the Institute of Management Accountants. This commission developed a framework of internal controls that has become the standard by which companies assess their compliance to the 1977 Foreign Corrupt Practices Act. The controls provide "reasonable assurances" around financial reporting, operating risks and compliance to laws and regulations.

In 2004, COSO published Enterprise Risk Management—Integrated Framework, expanding on their initial COSO framework. In 2006, COSO again expanded their framework to include Internal Control over Financial Reporting—Guidance for Smaller Public Companies. This directive is aimed at supporting smaller organizations in implementing adequate internal controls over financial reporting.

Financial Reporting and Data Implications

The data management program should address the following aspects of financial reporting:

- What specific data attributes contribute to financial reporting?
- Who owns the data and where is it?
- What is the data quality of the data and how can it be improved?
- Are the proper controls for access and management in place?
- How should we track the data as it moves along the financial reporting process?
- How far back in history should we keep the data for current financial statements?
- What compliance tracking metrics are necessary?
- What testing is appropriate to ensure controls for safeguarding data quality are effective?
- What data standards should be developed to ensure timely, accurate financial reporting?

The data attributes that make up financial reporting come from the firm's SEC form 10K or quarterly form 10Q documents, including its balance sheet, its income statement and other management disclosures. Working back from these documents, identify all the data attributes, including all the intermediate data attributes that contribute to the financial report.

Critical to financial reporting accuracy is the data quality of the incoming data. This requires a comprehensive data quality program for all critical data attributes. All contributors of critical data used in financial reporting data should ensure data quality programs are in place and have effective metrics and controls to validate the accuracy of the filing.

Managing the storing and archiving of data for financial reporting is another aspect of data management. Determining how far back in time the company may be required to report is a decision made by the CFO and validated by the firm's external auditor. History is then collected and stored using critical controls. Once data has exceeded its archive life, guidelines for how the information should be disposed of are documented. Ongoing monitoring that all the programs and procedures for data management are followed, including testing the data controls for effectiveness, will be necessary.

Every step in the end-to-end data transfer leading up to the financial report requires control to ensure that the data is moved from one step to another without incident, that data quality is maintained and that access to the data is strictly controlled.

Summary

Having an effective data management program is an important contributor to regulatory and legal compliance. However, compliance is not just a data function. It is up to the business owners, managers, executives and directors of the company to pool resources to establish a clearly defined compliance program with policies on how the information resources are to be accessed, controlled, managed, archived and stored. They must also see to it that corporate guidelines are documented and ensure that the organization as a whole is aware of the legal and financial consequences of mismanaging data. Establishing a separate information security organization and a chief privacy officer to be accountable for driving implementation are some of the key ways that corporations meet these challenges. The chief privacy officer or chief compliance officer will partner with the corporate data functions to implement a comprehensive data management program that satisfies the regulatory compliance needs.

Regulatory compliance procedures on the global front are not going to relax. In fact, we can count on these regulations becoming stricter over time if data breaches become more common. Make sure that your organization is fully briefed and up to date on the changes in this area. Failure to keep abreast of statutory rules and regulations may put you in the news or, worse still, in jail. Remember Enron and WorldCom.

The list of regulations for compliance that we've provided here is not comprehensive nor industry specific. It is only to illustrate the importance of educating yourself and your organization on the regulations around data, its use and maintenance. This list is courtesy of the *OnTrack Data Recovery Web site: http://www. ontrackdatarecovery.com/data-recovery-regulatory-compliance/ (2007).*

4

Data and Performance Measurement

Your CEO has just come back from the annual CEO conference. Her peers are professing the benefits of Business Performance Management (BPM) and she is anxious to create a corporate sales pipeline dashboard with KPI (Key Performance Indicator) metrics—from the top to bottom—for the company.

The company has suffered by not having true visibility into sales opportunities by product, by country and by division. This has caused her to misrepresent financial sales forecast numbers to the board. Equally frustrating are the numerous meetings with the CFO and the sales teams to reconcile the many sales reports each product group, country and division head brings into the monthly sales review. She has come to you because she has heard about your business leadership in driving the enterprise data management program.

While she has learned from her peers the many benefits of BPM, she has also been alerted there are many data pitfalls in creating a corporate dashboard and she wants to get it right the first time. You have agreed to come back in a few weeks with specific recommendations. Now what? What do you tell her?

What is Business Performance Management (BPM) Anyway?

In 1989, Howard Dresner, a research analyst at Gartner, popularized BPM as an umbrella term to describe a set of concepts, methods and applications to improve business decision-making by using fact-based support systems. Today the category of BPM has been expanded to include applications that align business priorities up and down the company through a common, end-to-end set of metrics that serve to optimize the execution of one or more business strategies. The term "business intelligence" has also been used to describe the application types in BPM.

In its infancy, business performance management applications were purely metric-centric applications that displayed the metrics for key daily or weekly performance indicators. Now these applications have matured to include more real-

Exhibit 4.1. Results Desired from BPM

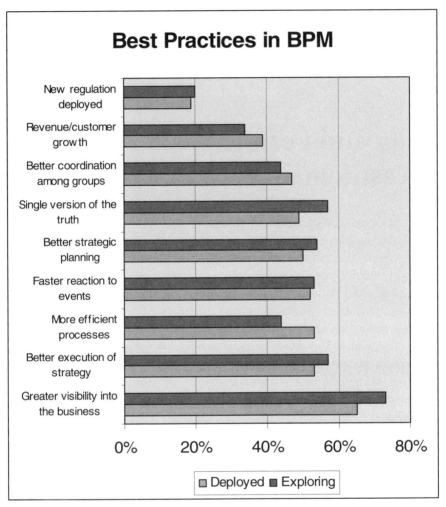

time process performance monitoring. Advance analytics and data mining are also being added to these applications. The analytics can evaluate the metrics and provide self-correcting actions, issue alerts, compare operational results to past history or compare results to pre-established targets, further aiding management decision-making.

Examples of Business Performance Management applications include:

- CEO-level balanced scorecards
- Tracking the sales opportunity pipeline through to a final customer order
- Tracking campaign effectiveness from planning to execution with mid-course correction capabilities

- Providing ongoing alignment of sales resources to profitable, high-growth accounts or markets
- Supply chain execution with inventory and logistic optimization
- Fraud detection

A March 2004 report on best practices in Business Performance Management by The Data Warehousing Institute (TDWI) cited the desired benefits and outcomes from BPM shown in Exhibit 4.1.

Most BPM applications are enterprisewide applications. A 2006 Knightbridge survey of 359 senior executives found a high degree of C-level involvement in business intelligence initiatives such as business performance management. C-level involvement is a sign of the business value of business performance management and a sign of how data is becoming a corporate asset that is so fundamental to decision-making. Deciding where to start is a key question. Those that have deployed BPM successfully advise to start out small with a focused project that can be implemented quickly and yet deliver results.

What Makes a BPM Application Difficult?

While there are many data challenges to creating a business performance management application, the biggest challenges, by far, are the business process and organizational cultural changes required to run the company with a common set of operational and business metrics. Aligning the entire company to a consistent set of metrics that adequately measures progress toward execution of the business strategy, with a consistent meaning for those metrics, a consistent process for evaluating the results and an integrated process for aligning companywide people, processes and assets to take correction actions is a HUGE undertaking. For that reason, successful BPM applications have strong top-down support from the CEO or the CFO. Oftentimes, as is the case with your CEO, the chief executive initiates the project because of a companywide pain point. As a result of the Sarbanes-Oxley Act, CFOs in particular have become key sponsors of BPM programs because of their responsibility to certify the operational soundness of a company's financial process. Very rarely does a BPM project start as a division-level project and grows to become the de facto companywide BPM application. It is just too hard to gain the necessary cross department agreements and resolve all the conflicting management agendas without strong top-down support. So, the first thing to tell your CEO is that her involvement will be required many times and in many ways. This will not be passive endorsement with a once a month project review. If she or one of her top lieutenants, like the CFO, is not willing to spend the necessary time on the project, then stop right there.

Data Challenges

Establishing an effective business performance management application with the appropriate executive scorecard, dashboards and reports requires integrating information that is scattered across many systems and processes to create a single version of the truth. This task alone will bring out new types of data issues that have lain dormant for decades. The data issues from this kind of integrating initiative are not unlike the 360-degree view of the customer issues that we discussed earlier.

Equally difficult is the requirement for real-time data reporting so that the metrics and information can be used to make effective business decisions in a timely manner. From a technical architecture perspective, a BPM application requires a turbocharged, resilient analytic environment for broad enterprise use. Data-mining runs scan through large volumes of current and history data to complete complex analysis. Once deployed and operational, many employees can access the system simultaneously, requesting additional reports and analysis. If not managed closely, ad hoc queries and reports run your application to a screeching halt, causing huge customer dissatisfaction and loss of confidence in the application. This is a big jump from the departmental business intelligence solutions most companies have implemented to date.

Adding to the technical performance challenges is the need to build a system that can adapt to changing business requirements. If the BPM application requires six to nine months to implement a new KPI or add a new data source or business process, it cannot keep up with the dynamic business changes.

One of the organizational challenges in deploying a BPM solution is ensuring adoption of the system by all users and developing the communication, processes, training and controls to ensure actions are taken with the data provided.

Here's a list of common data issues encountered during a BPM project:

- The same data mean different things across different applications.
- Ad hoc reporting and queries can cause performance havoc on a production environment if not isolated.
- Executives will not use the dashboard in operational meetings as is, but may rather ask their staff to run separate reports and measurements, creating their own "shadow" databases.
- Effective data mining and analytics requires historic data that is often not available. This can lead you to evaluate anew your archiving policies for data.
- Learning new data visualization techniques may be applicable across multiple mediums.

Twelve Steps to Making BPM Work

1. **Start with a good team.**

    Successful BPM teams allocate sufficient resources and hire top-notch people to deliver results consistently (see Exhibit 4.2).

    With the right team in place, successful BPM applications are possible.

Exhibit 4.2. Project Team Capabilities

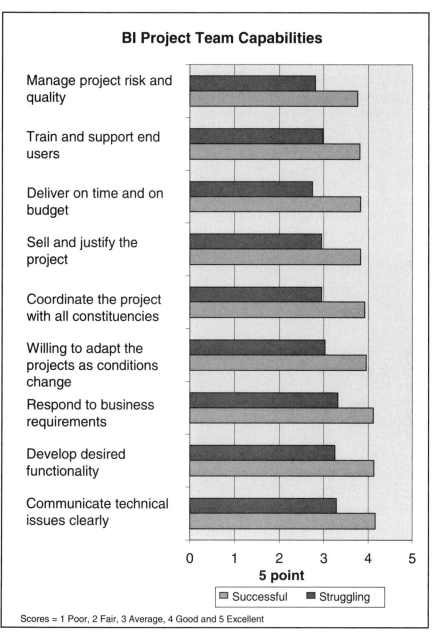

Source: *Smart Companies in the 21st Century: The secrets of creating successful business intelligence solutions,* TDWI Report Series, March 2004.

2. **Have STRONG top-down, visible and consistent support from the CEO and/or CFO.**

This can not be underestimated. Visible endorsement is required throughout the life of the project. In the beginning, this support ensures that competing division priorities and cross department management agendas don't derail the project. Once the program is operational, ensuring the appropriate funds are in place to keep the BPM application up to date and aligned with the changes in the business strategies is the next big imperative. Enforce the elimination of "rogue databases" developed clandestinely over time. Keep the discipline of using metrics and running the business using them.

Exhibit 4.3 shows the results of an April 2003 survey by TDWI of BI professionals who had deployed BI solutions plus interviews with BI experts, BI consultants, industry analyst, and BI solution. Successful BI projects have a high proportion of "very committed" sponsors.

Exhibit 4.3. Level of Sponsor Commitment

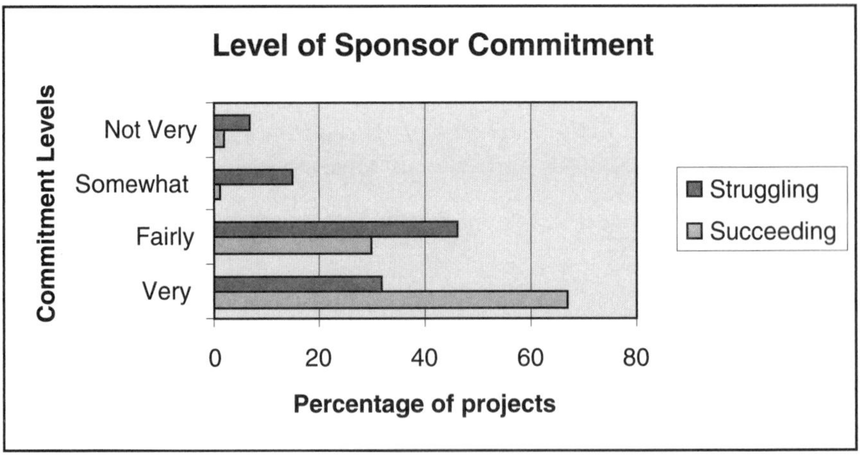

Source: *Smart Companies in the 21st Century: The secrets of creating successful business intelligence solutions,* TDWI Report Series, April 2003.

Sponsorship of the most successful projects happens at the highest levels, as shown in Exhibit 4.4.

Exhibit 4.4. Successful Sponsors

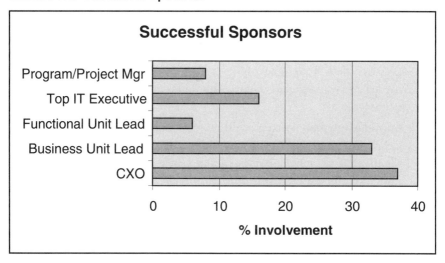

Source: *Smart Companies in the 21st Century: The secrets of creating successful business intelligence solutions*, TDWI Report Series, April 2003.

3. **Establish performance metrics jointly with business leaders, process leaders and data experts. Agree on the interim KPIs used to measure performance. This step takes time. Do not give up; be persistent.**
   Key performance indicators (KPIs) are financial, non-financial and operational metrics used to quantify the strategic performance of the organization. In BPM or business intelligence applications, KPIs are used to represent the state of the business by monitoring business processes and prescribe a course of action. When designing a KPI, think "SMART":
   - Specific
   - Measurable
   - Achievable
   - Realistic
   - Timely

Here are some examples of KPIs:
   - Status of the sales pipeline according to defined sales opportunity progression stages
   - Customer attrition over a specific period
   - New customers acquired over a period
   - Status of a customer order according to defined order progression stages

Involving the business, data and process experts in defining the metrics will ensure the KPI metrics are relevant to the business process being monitored and the metrics can be implemented. KPI metrics should also be easy to understand.

4. **Ensure common, clear definitions of the metrics that are understood by all parties.**

    Let's use the KPI examples above to demonstrate why clear definitions are needed and why even an obvious definition is not so obvious. Here are some examples:

    Customer attrition: What is a customer? Is it only an existing customer that has purchased recently? What about a prospect visiting your company Web site that did not purchase? What about a customer who has not purchased from the company for a long time? How many years should an inactive customer is considered a customer before they are considered to have been lost?

    Status of the sales pipeline according to defined sales opportunity progression stages: What are the sales opportunity progression stages? What event triggers the sales opportunity to move from one stage to another? What day do we use to pull the information—must be consistent across all opportunities?

    New customers acquired over a period: At what point is a customer considered "acquired"? When they place an order? When the order is delivered? When they pay the invoice? What about if they returned the order within 30 days? What about inactive customers returning from a long hiatus from purchasing with us?

    Status of a customer order according to defined order progression stages: Through what stages does an order progress? What event triggers the sales order to move from one stage to another? Is the order considered "sold" when the order is placed? When the order is delivered? When the order is paid? What does on-time delivery mean? When is the customer request delivered or when is the company's committed delivery time met?

    Taking the time to get clear definitions and agreements ensures success of your BPM application

5. **Establish the executive dashboard with no less than 70% automated input. Minimize manual entries.**

    Many BPM applications start out with the majority of their KPI metrics calculated or sourced from spreadsheets, manual reports or other non-structured data. Typically this occurs because these metrics are new and calculating them requires additional information not found in the traditional databases in the company. While this is an acceptable way to get started, it is not an acceptable model for running the business. Manual entries and spreadsheets create opportunities for data quality defects because of the potential for human errors. There is also more potential for control escapes and process break downs from employee risks. Keep a log of all the data inputs required in the BPM application and systematically automate these manual data sources. Achieving a 70% automated input to 30% manual ratio for data sources is an acceptable level. Getting to 100% is even better, of course, but what is often the case is some KPI metrics, especially financial forecast numbers, requires additional approvals or assessments before release.

6. **Establish ongoing communication with executives to ensure dashboards are being used as they are constructed and that ad hoc reporting is minimal.**
Division level executives have a tendency to want to see their business reports in a particular reporting format that suits their preferences. Enforcing a common companywide dashboard with common reports runs against their grain. What eventually happens is the division executive's staff begins to take the data from the BPM corporate database and create their own division-level databases, adding other metrics and other reports. Not only is this a wasteful replication of data, but over time erodes the adoption and usage of the common set of metrics. Your CEO should lead by example using only the BPM corporate dashboard and common reports to run her status meetings with her executives. Additionally, the BPM team should establish ongoing communication with the key executives to monitor their usage and address any issues they have toward using the common dashboard. The flexibility of the BPM applications today allows for customization of the data presentation to suit many different preferences.

7. **Establish executive dashboard drill-down capabilities from CEO to lowest level decision-makers.**
An effective BPM program has the capability to view the KPI metrics down to the lowest level of execution that is meaningful to that metric. That level can be a particular business process, a department level or a key decision-maker. As an example, for the sales opportunity dashboard desired by the CEO, the CEO and all her key executives should be able to view their contribution to the sales opportunity metrics down to a department level. The CEO sees an aggregated total for each division, but then sees the contribution also by product type, by country and state, and by department. By having this level of granularity, the sales executive teams can see non-performing products or regions in a timely manner. Corrective actions can be taken such as additional product discounts, targeted marketing campaigns or sales incentives. Of course, this level of drill down does not happen overnight. The more manual the data entry on the dashboard, the more time-consuming creating this capability will be. Creating extensive drill-down capability is another reason to automate the KPI metric calculation by ensuring all data sources are coming from structured databases.

8. **Ensure the executive dashboard uses the appropriate data visualization techniques.**

They say a picture is worth a thousand words and in an executive BPM dashboard that axiom takes on even greater significance. While many BPM applications start with standard reports and spreadsheet-looking scorecards, they can quickly advance to providing other visualization capabilities such as pie charts, line graphs, bar charts or color status indicators. Different visualization options allow individual metrics to be displayed with the best presentation format for that metric. Different visualization options also allow many metrics to be shown on one page or screen without the usual distracting lines and columns. Having these various presentation options addresses the executives' preferences for how they like to see their business performance reported.

Look at some examples of optimum presentation techniques for different metrics:

Customer Attrition
- Line graph showing monthly customer attrition over a 12-month period
- Bar chart showing current year and previous year attrition by month

Sales Opportunity by Stages
- Bar chart showing sales opportunity in each stage with actual, planned and prior year bars
- Table showing sales opportunity with actuals versus planned— Green/Red/Yellow indicating status
- Pie chart showing total sales opportunity by % in each stage

9. **Use the dashboard in operational meetings and provide guidelines to ensure management does not constantly ask drill-down questions of the troops.**

Ensuring your CEO, CFO and senior executives use the corporate BPM dashboard in their operational meetings drives rapid adoption of the tool as well as alignment of the metrics companywide. However, because the dashboard is providing real-time operational performance monitoring there can be a tendency to reach for the phone every time an executive sees a number on the dashboard he doesn't like or doesn't understand. This can quickly consume the staff and the front-line employees who should be spending more time with customers and not internal staff. Establish a companywide management system and process for how and when the metrics are to be reviewed and do not violate the process by asking questions outside the agreed upon review cadence. Even the CEO and CFO have to follow the process, as their off-the-cuff questions can be the ones that cause the most churn for the employees and staff. While keeping the CFO and CEO from not asking questions out of the process sounds impossible, it will minimize their questions to only the most critical ones that require an immediate response. Believe us, it is possible!

10. **Plan for rapid growth. Once the information becomes available and ingrained in the management system, users acquire an insatiable desire for more and more reports and metrics.**
    The catch phrase from the movie *Field of Dreams*—"Build it and they will come"—certainly applies to a corporate BPM program. This is especially clear to the organization when the CEO and senior executives use BPM. The management system becomes the place to go for companywide performance metrics. If this becomes the mode of operation in your company, plan for rapid growth and be flexible to changes as the metrics reflect changes in your company strategy or in business processes. The application must change quickly when the business changes. Being able to adapt to these changes quickly necessitates a flexible technical architecture and the levels of staffing to make changes quickly. Giving the business teams some capability to make changes on their own is also a good practice.

    While growth of metrics and their usage is good, there is also a danger of too many reports and too many metrics. Continually asking the question "How will you use the data?," can help eliminate unnecessary reporting. Ensuring that the data is used to better understand the business is your first task. This goal is helped by establishing common reports as much as possible, rather than generating a series of special, ad hoc reports for each unique request.

11. **Establish a governance process that includes business, process and data executive stakeholders for managing the program and evaluating new requirements, new usages and new KPI metrics.**
    After your CEO gives the authorization and funding to start the project, establish a management system to govern the program and run the governance forum. Name a senior executive, such as the CFO, to be the primary executive responsible for the implementation. The governance forum should include cross company business as well as process and data stakeholders. Successful governance manages the project deliverables, allocates resources, prioritizes projects and resolves issues. Once the initial project is deployed, the governance forum also manages the adoption and usage of the BPM dashboard.

    Name a constituent representative who can evaluate new user demands placed on a metric. Ensure "measurement" overload is not placed on one audience. For example, appoint a sales manager to evaluate all the metrics and reports on what a sales manager will receive. Make sure that he is comfortable with both the information that the report provides, but also the cadence of when he receives the report and the format. A good practice is to appoint someone who is in the line organization to play this role and not someone from a staff organization. Staff personnel, while well-intentioned, are far removed from the day-to-day sales activity and often do not appreciate the workload imposed by a myriad of reports or metrics.

TDWI survey respondents were asked how they ensured alignment of a BI solution. Their answers appear in Exhibit 4.5.

12. **Ensure accountability to KPI metrics.**
For the KPI metrics to take hold and to drive performance in the right direction, there must be accountability to the metrics at all levels of the company. In addition to top executive enforcement, carefully thought out compensation plans and incentive programs are needed.

Data Management Implications

Building a BPM program and solution may mean that you need to leverage all of the tools or data management programs that you have put in place. In fact, if there is a common theme to this book, it is that an enterprise data management program benefits many other processes and re-engineering efforts. That is, given its broad

Exhibit 4.5. How to Ensure Alignment

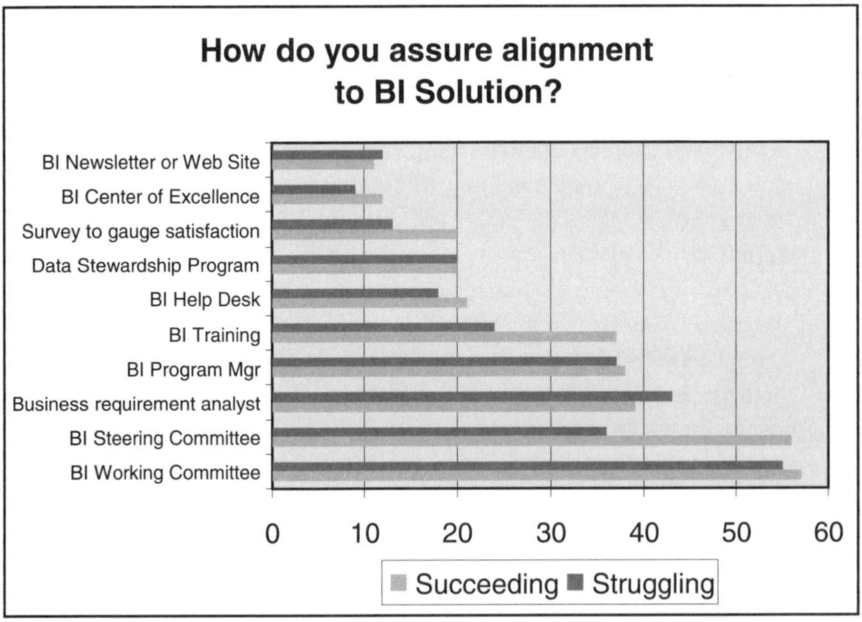

Source: *Smart Companies in the 21st Century: The secrets of creating successful business intelligence solutions*, TDWI Report Series, March 2004.

benefits and capabilities, an enterprise data management program helps increase the success of other initiatives such as BPM. A BPM project should use the following parts of the enterprise data management program.

Leverage the Common Data Business Terms

Defining common KPI metrics is foundational to BPM programs. Once KPI metrics are defined the next step is decomposing the metrics into all the contributing data attributes that make up the metric and finding all the databases that have those attributes in all the company databases. This job becomes a whole lot easier if the company has a companywide data model with consistent business data terms and values defined in the corporate data dictionary. New KPI terms should be added to the data model if appropriate, but at a minimum added to the corporate data dictionary.

Leverage the Enterprise Metadata

The enterprise metadata is catalogued database information (data models, data attributes, allowable values, physical structures, data quality level, owner). Once KPI metrics and contributing data attributes are identified, finding and collecting the metrics across all the company databases and systems would be a daunting task if not for an enterprise metadata. For those data attributes not found in the enterprise metadata, then this data will be new. The source for the new data attributes will be determined to be either a manual process or created new in a database. Certainly the latter is preferable. The new BPM database should use all the enterprise data standards and its database information logged in the enterprise metadata.

Leverage the Data Quality Programs

Having high-quality data as input into the KPI metrics produce high-quality KPI metrics. The converse is also true, low data quality produces low-quality KPI metrics. Making important business strategy decisions with low-quality data is dangerous. Therefore good data quality is critically important for a successful BPM program. Any and all data quality initiatives positively affect the BPM program. The enterprise metadata catalogues the data quality of the contributing data attributes. As the BPM solution is being designed, an assessment should be made on the data quality of the contributing data attributes. An aggressive data quality program may be required before or in parallel to the BPM application deployment.

As the BPM program becomes a "mission critical" process for running the company, the data attributes that contribute to the KPI metrics should be classified as "critical data attributes" in the enterprise metadata. As a critical data attribute, appropriate key controls and ongoing data quality programs should be instituted.

Leverage the "Trusted Sources" of Data

You know that the information that you enter into your own contact database is as accurate as you know at any given time. But what do you know about the "trustworthiness" of the data that's entered into the systems in your company? Which ones could be "trusted" sources of information? Here are some questions to ask yourself about the sources that you depend on each day.

- Do the applications where data is entered allow for data to be checked for accuracy before entry? What data quality checks are performed?
- How timely are the updates of this information?
- Is data entry a dedicated responsibility of someone's job or just something added to their regular job role?
- Is someone assigned to manage the quality of the data in this source?

The sources that will command your trust are those that return reliable, quality information consistently.

If you don't have an enterprise data management program in place, BPM is a great reason to start. Target the new enterprise data management program with addressing the data challenges of BPM.

Summary

The reason that Business Performance Management (BPM) is gaining popularity among senior executives is that it closely aligns a company's operational metrics to its business strategy. Then, it helps executives monitor the execution of these metrics in real time with timely corrective actions. Your CEO was right, there are many benefits to BPM and there are many challenges. But now you know what they are and can report back to your CEO about how to make your BPM program a success. If you still have not implemented an enterprise data management program, look to BPM to give you and your colleagues the impetus to start one. BPM is a great reason!

5

Growing and Managing a Data Culture

Your company data is the foundation on which you base your business decisions. Keeping it at a quality level not only helps you comply with external governance, but also helps you better understand how your company is performing. It is in short the building block on which the growth and performance of your company is based.

So why then do so few companies actually have an active data management culture? Because most companies, like people, have a hierarchy of needs. If a company's needs are being filled, then it doesn't perceive that it needs to do anything about its data. Data is so fundamental to the fabric of a company that its care is often taken for granted. Similar to electricity and running water, most companies just expect data to be available without much intervention.

Let's understand how the data needs of the firm evolve by using a well known, time-tested self-development model—Maslow's Hierarchy of Needs. Parallels exist between an individual's self-development stages as defined in Maslow's hierarchy of human needs and an organization's data development stages. Let's look at a Hierarchy of Data Needs and consider that the company has not yet made the complete change to a data-driven culture until it reaches "self-actualization." Understanding where your company is in the stages of data needs helps pinpoint the culture changes necessary at each of these stages.

To help us completely understand how to apply Maslow's hierarchy to a data environment, let's begin with a preview of what Maslow had in mind.

A Hierarchy of Human Needs

Abraham Maslow was an American psychologist in the 1940s. He is best known for his proposal on the hierarchy of human needs and the theory of human motivation. Maslow used his theory to explain the development of mankind through multiple stages of motivation, ultimately resulting in the final stage of "self actualization." His Hierarchy of Needs states we must satisfy each need in order, starting with the most basic needs. Only when the lower, most basic needs are satisfied can individuals concern themselves with the higher needs of esteem and personal growth. Furthermore, once we arrive at the higher needs, if circumstances eliminate any of the most basic needs, then we are no longer concerned with the maintenance of the higher human needs, but rather act to remove the deficiency. An example of the theory plays out when a serious illness affects a high-charging executive. As a person progresses in their career and achieves financial and professional success, they begin to think about fulfilling philanthropic goals and leaving a legacy. However, if at this stage a serious illness befalls the executive, his priorities shift to the most basic need of getting well and providing for the future of his family.

The hierarchy of needs can also be used to explain personal and organizational motivation. While motivation does not change behavior, it is one of the factors that can lead to new behaviors. Behaviors are influenced by motivation, but also by culture, biology and situational factors. As such, understanding the motivations in each of the stages can be used to understand and thus begin to change organizational behavior around data.

The Human Needs Pyramid

In his definitive work in 1943, Maslow wrote that humans are perpetually "want animals." All needs are instinctive, with some more powerful than others. He arranged the human needs in order of their potency—the lower in the pyramid, the more instinctive and powerful (see Exhibit 5.1). No need or motivation can be treated as if it exists in an isolated or discrete way. Every drive is related to the state of satisfaction or dissatisfaction of other drives. The first four layers of the pyramid are called "deficiency needs." Satisfying these needs does not create "satisfaction," it simply eliminates anxiety. Once satisfied, however, the needs after the deficiency needs *do* create satisfaction and motivation.

Biological and physical needs. Biological and physical needs include basic life needs—air, food, drink, shelter, warmth, sex, sleep, etc. These are the most potent of all needs. A person who lacks food, safety, love and esteem would want food more strongly than anything else. All human capacities and behaviors are focused on hunger satisfaction. Capacities that are not useful for this purpose are pushed to the background. The person's perspective of the ideal future state is absorbed by the need to fulfill these basic needs. An extremely hungry man tends to think he will be perfectly happy if food is guaranteed for life. The theory claims, however, that once the hunger need is satisfied, that want is no longer a want. The motivations and behaviors of the individual then focus on the next unsatisfied need.

Safety needs. Safety needs come immediately after basic comfort needs. Assuming that the physiological needs are well gratified, the need to secure basic safety needs becomes apparent. These needs include protection, security, order, law, limits, stability, etc. All that was said before about the dominating behaviors and thoughts produced by the lack of fulfillment of these needs is true here as well, but to a somewhat lesser degree. A person who feels chronically unsafe will live for safety alone. A lack of routine or predicable order in a person's life can also cause feelings of anxiety and safety-need deficiency. A broader interpretation of the need for safety and stability is the need for a "world" philosophy or a grand strategy, sometimes addressed with religion or other organizing goals. The need for safety is an active stimulant to behavior in times of war, natural catastrophes, crime waves and chronically bad situations.

Belonging needs. If both the physiological and safety needs are fairly well met, then the belonging needs emerge. The belonging needs include love, family, affection, relationships, and work groups and the need to be accepted. The person feels the absence of belonging as never before. Love needs involve both giving and receiving love.

Esteem needs. All humans in our society have a need to be respected by others and more importantly themselves. Achievement, status, responsibility, reputation are examples of the esteem need. Satisfaction of the self-esteem need leads to feelings of self-confidence, worth, strength, of being useful and necessary in the world. When these needs are not met, they produce feelings of inferiority, weakness and helplessness.

Self-actualization needs. Finally, after all other needs are met, the desire for personal growth and fulfillment becomes important. To be all that a person can be, to realize one's potential, is the ultimate need of humans. The specific form that these needs take will vary greatly by person. The self-actualization need also includes connecting to something beyond the ego or beyond helping others find their potential. As a person becomes more self-actualized, they become wiser and they know what to do in a wide variety of situations.

Exhibit 5.1. A Hierarchy of Human Needs

Exhibit 5.2. A Hierarchy of Data Needs

A Hierarchy of Data Needs

Maslow's theory remains valid today for understanding human motivation, management training and personal development. The model can also be used to explain the evolutionary needs of data within an organization and to predict the next level of data development needs. Business and data managers can assess where they are in their data maturity needs and prioritize actions to address the most pressing need. Even more important is using the theory to prevent the organization from jumping through the needs before sufficiently addressing all the basic ones.

The Data Needs Pyramid

Biological and physical needs. The equivalent "food, water and air" of data needs is the basic raw data required by employees in the firm to do their job. At this basic level, the data can come from many sources and in many different formats. Employees are not demanding formality or processes in gathering the data they need. They just need the data.

The various basic repositories where data resides are obviously the corresponding "shelter" for the data within your company. Data exists in repositories such as reports, paper documents, spreadsheets or structured databases. At this stage the repositories are simple and basic. Little enhancement of the data is done for usability, analytics or the sake of quality. "Just give me the data" is the norm. The information needs at this low level are simple. The data is used to manage the most basic of job functions. As an example, a sales employee's basic data needs would be her customer's name, contact information and perhaps what the customer last purchased. With this basic data a salesperson can perform the sales jobs of contacting a customer. The salesperson can acquire this information from her manager, from a report or even from the phone book. The sales rep doesn't care which of these sources provide the information, she just cares that the information is correct. When she calls James Smith from XYZ Corporation, she doesn't want to hear that she really wants to talk to Jimmy Smythe. A shipping clerk's basic data needs include the customer's name, address and what items need to be shipped. He can acquire this data from an order form, an invoice or an online order entry database.

This data provides the bare essentials that the sales rep and the order entry clerk need to do their jobs. Just as food, water and air are essential for survival, accurate data is essential for these individuals to survive in their jobs.

Safety needs. The data needs at the safety stage include data protection, data consistency, data quality, data security, data order (process), data law (standards), data limits (valid values) and data stability.

Once an organization has satisfied the basic data needs of its employees, concerns and questions arise about the safety and security of the data being used. As the sales representative and the data entry clerk start to use the data in their daily jobs, concerns and questions arise over the security and stability of the data they need. For example, here are some of the questions the sales rep may have as she starts to use the data that describes her customers:

- How do I know this customer and contact number are correct?
- How do I know if someone else has contacted this customer?
- How do I prevent others from contacting my customer or making changes to my customer account information without informing me?
- How do I make a change to the account data in an orderly manner such as not to disrupt an existing customer order?
- What is the best method to contact this customer? Do I have their permission to send email?
- Can I share this data with my other vendors and contractors that might be servicing this account?

Likewise, the order entry clerk may have similar questions:

- How do I know that this is the correct shipping address and not just the address of the person who signed the purchase order?
- How can I make sure that the correct SKUs were assigned to this order?
- What are the terms and conditions of this order? Should it be shipped now or held for other pieces?
- Can I share this information with our distributor?

As data safety needs surface, employees seek data that helps them gain better information about their data. As you can see, they also start to raise questions about others who might want to use the data and how they can ensure that the data they receive is kept consistent and available to them. They begin to seek assistance in ensuring their data is safe and secure. In addition, they may also want more formal approaches to the data and more organized ways to access it.

At this stage, the firm's need for a higher level strategy for data begins to emerge. That is, they begin to realize that they need someone to help "watch over" critical data that is used by one or more departments. Individual departments or functions begin to implement their own specific department databases and their own data quality checks. In more enlightened organizations, some form of a data stewardship role emerges. Here you also see the firm's desire to keep personal identifiable information (PII) more secure and processes around data privacy and security begin to be articulated.

But as history has shown, once a civilization can take care of its basic needs for food, water, clothing and shelter, often the next stage is to secure your resources for yourself. This basic need for security leads to building moats, walls and other secure devices. In the world of data, it leads to each organization building its own data repository. This stage is also the beginning of data anarchy. With each department building its own data repository to solve its requirements, the opportunity for data to be duplicated in each of these repositories is immense. This leads to "data states," unique islands of data with their own terminology, definitions and processes. Now the sales representative has a field in her database called "customer" that doesn't match the field in the order entry database named "customer."

The safety stage is a great time to start the Enterprise Data Management program. If you can catch departments when they start to build their individual data repositories, then you can begin to introduce good data management practices and consistency across organizations. Unfortunately, this is also one of the most difficult stages in which to start an enterprise data program. Usually the organization is not yet mature enough to realize the need for an enterprise way of solving data issues. For each department, speed of implementation is critical and the need to control their individual environments and destinies is paramount. "They know best" what is required of their data and they will handle it. The leaders of the enterprise data management program can count on encountering massive resistance to any kind of enterprisewide program.

In order to successfully launch an enterprise data management program at this stage, the organization needs VERY strong executive sponsors. Direct involvement of the CEO or CFO is required to launch the program, squelch resistance and foster collaboration. At this stage, the leaders of the enterprise data management program need to allocate sufficient time to educate and communicate on the importance of the solving data issues at the enterprise level. Just as kings, emperors and presidents strive to bring together separate city states and factions, the data leaders at the enterprise level within an organization need to be prepared for battles, victories, defeats, compromises and ultimately treaties.

Belonging needs. Data belongings needs refer to the firm's desire for a higher level of data organization, data relationship and data working groups.

The data program of individual departments and functions do not satisfy the needs of data for the entire organization. However, these data approaches have probably already been well entrenched in the different departments and centered around that department's specific data requirements. As the organization grows, its requirement for using data across processes also grows. The need to share data is often the driving force behind the next level in the hierarchy of data needs—belonging. Evidence that your company is in this stage can be seen in the number of re-engineering projects that you have. Take a look around. Do you have a CRM, ERP, or KPI scorecard project funded for this year? Are you grappling with how to take advantage of online commerce? These kinds of projects will quickly bring to the surface issues associated with data. If no one group is stepping up to solve these problems holistically, then the problem is more difficult to solve.

At this stage, the sales and order entry departments and the company as a whole are now ready for an enterprise data management program. They see the errors of their current ways and the need for a coordinated approach to data quality and management. At this point, there is a strong need for a Chief Data Officer. Usually at this stage, the proliferation of data projects may have already caused broad data challenges. Acting swiftly to rein in the various departmental approaches and to establish a role for a data officer helps to bring together the data community. At this stage of belonging, community is what the data organizations need and it gives you a perfect opportunity to launch enterprise programs for stewardship, data quality, enterprise metadata and common data definitions. At this point, you can begin to implement a data architecture designed to share data across databases.

Prioritizing where to start is the key challenge at this stage. Resistance to enterprise data management can come from the prioritization process, as each executive's favorite data project finds itself at the top of the priority list with an "immediate" tag appended to it. Like fiefdoms coming together under the king, these groups may want to unite for strength, but not give up their own lands. In other words, they want to be part of the data kingdom, but do not want to lose control over their own data. If the data organization allows individual data projects to continue, they should, at a minimum, be done within the framework of common data methodologies, use common data tools, employ an enterprise metadata model and follow common data standards. The data management team may be required to write Database Principles to bring factions together.

This stage also requires sufficient time for education and communication. While the organization may be ready for enterprise data management, it won't necessarily understand what that means to specific roles within the various organizations. Building a department responsible for data management within a company often leads other departments to assume that they have no responsibility for managing data. They feel that all data issues will be solved by the Chief Data Officer and her team. Nothing is further from what needs to happen. Clearly articulating and communicating responsibilities for data across the business, leads to better community and better data over time.

In Maslow's hierarchy, the belonging stage highlights the need for developing relationships. Building data relationships are equally important at this stage. Creating a forum for building common enterprise data priorities and aligning the enterprise data strategy with individual organizational projects is an important part of this relationship building. Steering committees, user groups, and stewardship councils are all examples of relationship building forums that can help build communities and give individuals a sense of belonging.

The skills and traits required of an effective enterprise data management organization at this stage include:

- communication and negotiation
- strong data quality and enterprise data architecture competencies
- understanding of the core business processes and how data management can support them
- experienced project management of large projects
- extensive process re-engineering, change management experience
- persistence

A strong executive sponsor helps ensure adoption and acceptance across the firm. In the previous security stage, sponsorship from the CEO or CFO was mandatory. In this stage, it is helpful, but not required. Allowing a senior executive to lead the data management councils and teams is often sufficient.

Esteem needs. Literally translated, esteem needs for data include data achievement and status (metrics), data responsibility (business process value) and data reputation (data integrity).

At this stage, the enterprise data management program is in operation, business data stewards are active participants in defining and implementing business processes and the firm has a sufficient level of trust in its data. The organization's data needs now shift to getting more integrated data faster in order to make better decisions. The need for real-time data to support corporate performance management dashboards and corporate key indicators emerge. Data is beginning to move from a purely operational, auxiliary function to a source for new growth opportunities. Data is also used to monitor and trend business performance. Data stewards move from an operational data quality focus to a trusted data advisor to business leaders.

In this stage, there is little resistance to the enterprise data management programs because EDM is working. However, new skills are required in the data organization to satisfy new data needs:

- expertise in real-time data architecture
- expertise in data mining and advanced analytics
- experience in companywide business process management and business intelligence projects
- enterprise data warehouse management

As you can probably guess, many companies jump to this level before they have successfully satisfied the needs of the previous stages. BPM is one of the hottest words in the business lexicon today. And real-time data is something that nearly every company with a Web site is trying to harness. But trying to take on these complicated, higher level needs is similar to trying to achieve the Nobel Prize for literature without knowing how to write.

Jumping into management of data on a real-time basis without completely building out the technical and process capabilities or meeting the needs of the stages before is a formula for disaster. For example, real-time data requires an enterprise data management data quality program that captures data quality issues at their point of creation and corrects them there. If the company's data quality program is designed around catching quality issues after the data has flowed into a data warehouse, then managing solutions that require real-time quality data is impossible. Real-time data also necessitates that the firm follow common definitions for similar business terms. This enables data to move seamlessly from one application to another to enable real-time transactions. Skipping these steps leads to failure.

Self-actualization needs. Data is regarded as a strategic asset for the firm because it is trusted, available and timely. Consistent data definitions allow for end-to-end process integration of all the firm's business processes, beginning with the basic ones of customer relationship and supply chain management. Daily business performance is monitored with good, real-time data. Now what? What more can the firm want from the enterprise data organization?

At this stage, the organization's data needs shift to wanting analysis capabilities integrated into its processes. No longer is a daily dashboard or report sufficient. The business now requires that data be available whenever it is needed, wherever it is wanted. For example, the sales rep now gets notified on her mobile device when her customer places an order. She can communicate via the same mobile device to the order entry clerk who can tell her immediately when the order will be shipped. And then she can see how that order contributes to her sales quota for the month. And all of this happens while she's in the field with another customer. Very few organizations have reached this level of enterprise data capability, but many strive for it. Sadly, many organizations attempt to put this kind of solution in place without going through the hierarchy of data needs. Thinking that the system is the answer, they develop systems that manage processes, but that still display inaccurate data that is not useful to those who need it.

But if a company were to reach the self-actualized stage of the data hierarchy, it might have these qualities:

- Data is spontaneous—real-time—available when and where it is needed.
- Data analysis and data mining have grown across the firm.
- Data quality is undisputed. High data quality is pervasive.
- Data is used to create new growth opportunities and is always the first item discussed when new strategies are being developed.
- Data alerts are in place so that employees receive automatic, personalized notification of changes to the data.

Determining where your company is on the Hierarchy of Data Needs is a critical step toward developing a data management culture. Implementing the programs that will help you manage a data culture is what we will take you through step by step in the remaining chapters of the book.

Implementing a Data Management Culture

Over the last five years, data management at the enterprise level has grown in popularity for companies around the world. As discussed earlier, regulatory requirements such as Sarbanes-Oxley, data privacy breaches and large corporate re-engineering efforts have all help contribute to the drive toward enterprise data management. Companies are realizing that having islands of department level data does give them the timely access or control to the data that they need in order to promote greater levels of integration within the company. While regulation and re-engineering may be driving this enterprise data management, good EDM benefits all critical company processes.

Unfortunately for most companies that have been in business for any length of time, years of neglect have created many data issues. Resolving these issues cannot and will not happen overnight. The good news is that the issues CAN be fixed and with an emphasis on data management, they can be fixed as quickly as the organization can come together around a data initiative.

Because most companies are just starting their enterprise data management efforts, we do not know of any company that has reached the optimal level of information maturity, as measured by the company's complete satisfaction and confidence with the state of the data that runs its business. There are, however, select and enlightened companies in all industries that do recognize the importance of good data and invest accordingly. Generally, in most companies, there is still much to do. Here are six steps that we believe should take you to an actualized data management company:

1. **Start at the top.** Engage an influential senior executive sponsor to help manage this data initiative.

2. **Manage data as a corporate asset.** Integrated into the overall fabric of your company, data should be viewed as a valuable asset.

3. **Deploy enterprise data management in stages** as information management needs grow. Remember the Hierarchy of Data Needs. You can't be self-actualized unless you can first satisfy the basic level of needs. In most companies, the safety needs are where you will mostly likely start. Starting with a small data quality program is the basic step. Then, move to larger, more company-wide programs.

4. **Establish accountability and governance.** Ensuring that everyone looks at data and its quality as part of their job is an ongoing issue with data management programs. Establish data leaders across the firm and governance forums that help manage this process.

5. **Get the right talent.** The right talent starts with getting the right person in charge of data. Whether it's a Chief Data Officer or someone who is passionate about building a data quality program, getting these people in the right places in the organization is imperative to your success.

6. **Communicate, educate, sell and overcome resistance.** One of the first lessons of business is that it's not always the best product that wins in the market, but the one that sells the most. That "truth" applied to your data quality program means that you have to continually communicate, educate and sell the idea of data quality. You will need resources—both money and people—to secure your quality projects. To get those, you will have to sell.

Summary

Changing technology is the easiest change to make. After all, technology changes are ultimately digital changes, that is, zeroes and ones coded by smart programmers in your company. Technology changes are also the easiest to maintain. Once the new databases, the enterprise metadata, and the new data tools are in production, keeping the machines and code running is straightforward. Ensuring the technology is used properly can be handled through employee education. Ensuring the enterprise metadata is kept current can be handled with processes and controls that ensure the metadata is complete. So far, so good.

Changing business processes to deliver high-quality data is more challenging. While there are certainly tools and methodologies that facilitate defining the new data management processes within the business processes, there is still that pesky human element. New processes have to be designed in a collaborative manner with people who can implement the process and be responsible for the process. Once a human element is brought into the change process, all the dynamics that come from resistance to change need to be addressed. So we are back to changing the culture as the key driver of sustainability of business process changes.

Changing employees' behaviors to treat data as a corporate asset IS the most difficult to sustain as it involves changing attitudes, perceptions and ultimately actions.

In the case of changing behaviors around data management, here are a few observable behaviors and situations that give you a hint that the culture is changing for the better:

- Data is used to grow the business, not just operate the business.
- There is no more finger pointing about "bad data."
- All employees take their data role seriously.
- Terms like trusted sources, enterprise metadata and enterprise data management are common vocabulary terms for all employees.
- Ongoing data quality and business intelligence investments are funded.
- Business intelligence is used to create new ways to look at your business.

All great journeys have a beginning and an end. But, as motivational leader Stephen Covey suggests in *The 7 Habits of Highly Successful People*, begin with the end in mind.

SECTION II

Making Data Work for You

Building and managing a quality data environment can be a daunting challenge. The next few chapters outline a process that helps:

1. Start at the top (Chapter 7).
2. Manage data as a company asset (Chapter 8).
3. Deploy enterprise data management in stages (Chapter 9).
4. Establish accountability and governance (Chapter 10).
5. Get the right talent (Chapter 11).
6. Communicate, educate, sell and overcome resistance (Chapter 12).

Enterprise data management is a relatively new management function, so the tools, processes and technologies that enable the function are still developing. With over thirty years of successes and setbacks to our credit, we have developed what we believe are best practices. Throughout the remainder of the book, we provide you with a complete set of those best practices. We do not expect your company to implement all these initiatives. Your best business judgment should help you pick the ones that work with your company's culture and can resolve your company's data pain points.

Let's begin your quest to improve your company's data environment with a tale about "bad data." It's a fictionalized compilation of situations drawn from stories we've collected over the years. If you recognize your company or your problems in the next chapter, then the information that follows should be just the right remedy for the issues you face.

6

The Ballad of "Bad Data"

The Data's Bad!

"The data's bad." The regional vice president of sales spoke directly into her desk telephone. She leaned closer as her voice rose and she practically shouted at the team of finance people on the conference call. "The data's not right! I know for a fact that we sold 14 units of our latest product into that company last week. What do you mean we're showing a negative sales number for the month end?"

"Margaret, we pulled the data just this morning," the finance manager said, trying to calm the rising tensions. "The figures might be slightly off, but not enough to make up for the difference you say it must be. Let us go back and take a look at how we accounted for the region's returns this month."

Placated for the moment, Margaret agreed but immediately called in her own operations team. "Wally, why are the figures that we're showing for sales last month so drastically different from what the finance team says we did?"

Wally could tell that the answer to this question would be very important. He also knew what lay at the heart of the problem. But what was the best way to tell his boss that the customer relationship management (CRM) system that the information technology department had just installed did not feed the information about sales bookings directly to the finance system? Each week a sales support person on his team took the bookings from the sales system and manually entered them into the finance system. But Sue, the sales assistant assigned that task, had been out on family leave for six weeks and the entry of sales bookings had fallen behind. That was only one of the problems. Sue had also had issues, before she left on leave, with matching the sales transactions to the right customers in the financial system. She had already explained to Wally how she had spent 25 hours in overtime during the last quarter end trying to tie the customers that the sales representatives listed on their orders with those listed in the financial systems. It had been a difficult and often confusing task.

Wally answered Margaret with a slight apology in his voice. "Well, the data could be better, but let's see if my team and I can get to the root cause of this 'bad' data. Give us this quarter and let us figure out how we can improve on this."

Although not happy, Margaret acquiesced. Wally had bought himself 90 days, but he knew that he'd have to get to the heart of the issue quickly.

Wally's Dilemma

Ninety days! Only three months! Wally sat at this desk with his head in his hands staring at the quarterly sales report. What had he been thinking when he asked Margaret for just a quarter to solve this problem. How could he have been so stupid? This data quality issue was not going to be easy to solve. Somehow, in the next 90 days, he had to identify what was really going on with the data and put it in terms that the executives would understand. And he had to get the issue raised to the executive level without causing a war between finance and sales. He had to ensure that all the executives involved could see how managing this data was important to not only the reports they needed, but to external regulations like Sarbanes-Oxley as well.

"What's the problem, Wally?" Alice, his new administrative assistant, poked her head into his office. "Are you okay?"

"No," Wally admitted. "I've just committed myself to the most undoable task in our company's history. I told my boss that I'd have an answer to our data issues before the end of this quarter. I don't even know where to start."

"How about I get you a cup of coffee?" Alice was too new to understand the gravity of the situation, but she offered some advice along with the coffee. "You know, there's a new Chief Data Officer in the company. I just saw the announcement about her appointment on the company Web site this morning. Do you think she might be able to help?"

Wally brightened, but looked at her puzzled. "What's a Chief Data Officer? I never heard of such a thing. What did the announcement say that she's supposed to do?"

"It said that she was going to help all departments understand the value of the data that their businesses depend on for decision-making. I think it also said that she would be starting with the finance department."

Alice retreated to get Wally's coffee and the internal phone extension for the new Chief Data Officer. When she returned she said, "Her name is Caroline O'Keefe. Should I get you on her calendar?"

"Please do. And right away," Wally said urgently. He sipped at his coffee and contemplated the issues. He thought what he needed was a system that would ensure that customer names and addresses were maintained for every department. If someone could do that for him, then he and Sue, his sales assistant, could more easily check customer names against a master record. That way he wouldn't have the sales for the quarter being booked against different regions because the names of the companies weren't matched.

Alice appeared again at his door. "Caroline is here to see you," she said, stepping back to let a short, slightly graying woman through the office door.

"So good to meet you," Caroline O'Keefe said with a generous, sincere smile as she extended her hand. "I understand from Alice that you have a problem that might need my help."

"Do I ever," Wally said, shaking her hand and offering Caroline a chair. "Thanks for being so available. I really could use your help on a situation that came up this morning during our weekly sales update call." Wally paused to catch his breath and maneuvered his computer so that Caroline could see the charts that had caused the issue.

"We presented these numbers for our regional sales to Bill Blackstone, our Worldwide Sales VP, this morning," Wally continued. "Finance was on the call, too. The problem was our numbers didn't jibe with finance. Our figures for this quarter were off from finance's numbers by $10.2M." The gravity of the situation struck Wally anew and he ran his fingers through his hair. "I don't know what happened. Can you help me?"

Caroline was thoughtful. "What do you suspect is the issue?"

"I think it may have something to do with the new CRM system that we've put in place," Wally offered. "It went online in the middle of this quarter and we've been having a hard time getting reports out of the system. When we do, the reports show numbers that we don't understand. My staff and I spend half of our time lately checking all the reports to ensure that our sales are reflected correctly. We've caught several problems with sales territory assignments. We also think that the accounting systems in finance may have company names listed differently than our systems. But, whatever the reason for the problem, I have only 90 days to fix it."

"Well, I'm not sure that 90 days is long enough to fix the problem," Caroline admitted. "But we can begin to identify where the issue is and derive a solution. From my 15 years of experience, it will take 90 days to get this problem recognized, agreed to and supported by executive management. Data quality issues need champions. Are you willing to be one?" she asked directly.

"Me?" Wally chuckled. "I have no choice. When my boss turned to me this morning during the call, I became the champion whether I wanted to be or not."

"Good," said Caroline. "Then we should start with the basics: Map the business process then evaluate the quality of the data that supports the process at each stage. After we've gotten all of that together, we'll begin the hard part—getting the fix for the issue on Margaret's agenda."

"Oh, that should be no problem," Wally said. "She's adamant that this be fixed."

"We'll see," said Caroline. "I just want to make sure that once we've identified the issues and the fix that we put a system in place that keeps it fixed. I'm glad to be working with you, Wally."

As she stood and walked toward the door, Wally asked quietly, "So you think it's possible that we could have a fix identified in 90 days?"

"I think we have to try. Let's start tomorrow with an all-day meeting between your team and mine."

The Ninety-Day Project

It had been a long 90 days. Wally and Caroline had worked together closely to ensure that the data issues had been identified, quantified and collated into a rational presentation for Wally's executive management. Now they both were cloistered in Caroline's conference room putting the finishing touches on the presentation they would make to Wally's management tomorrow.

"Thanks for all your help over the past few months, Caroline." Wally was tired, but confident that the work he and Caroline had done would show the executive team that the issues needed more attention than just these past 90 days.

"I think we've done a good job of identifying which applications have been causing the issues and what we need to do to improve our matching of company names between systems. But I'm still not sure that we have executive support to maintain the focus on these issues."

"I spoke with Margaret yesterday," Wally continued. "I wanted her to know that we would be pointing out that the problems did not just reside in one organization. Each organization needs to share part of the problem and become part of the solution. It was clear from her expression that she was looking for a cleaner answer, but I held my ground."

"That's the hardest hurdle for management to overcome," Caroline said as she shifted in her seat. "The first reaction to data quality problems is usually a quick and urgent command: Just fix it! After they realize that 'just fixing it' may solve only some temporary pains, they are overcome often by the complexity and enormity of the job ahead. It takes courage to tackle these kinds of issues because it can take years to see substantial benefits."

"I've been thinking about that," Wally said. "Suppose we could start to illustrate concrete ways that the data is being used today. Wouldn't that help us sell our projects better?"

"Of course it would," Caroline said. "We need to illustrate in a positive manner all the uses of quality data—how data contributes to the company's view of our customer and how important that data is to managing the business. That should be our next project. What do you think about changing our last slide in tomorrow's presentation to highlight these actions as our next steps?"

"That's a great idea," Wally said, reaching for the slides that lay on the conference room table. "Let's make that our next 90-day agenda."

Nine Months Later

Wally's executive manager, Margaret, sat at the end of the long conference table, an area vice president of sales on either side of her. Wally sat to her right and listened as Caroline wrapped up her presentation at the front of the conference room. Caroline and Wally had worked hard alongside one another for over nine months and had finally begun to see the results of their work. Caroline had joined Margaret's staff meeting today to give her monthly update on the projects that Wally and she had been managing.

". . . and the monthly dashboard that you and your team have been receiving will be updated this next month to include a ranking of all sales representatives by share of quota achieved. I'm sure that you'll find it helpful. My team and I are looking forward to your feedback so that we can continue to improve on it." Caroline clicked her presentation to reveal her final slide then turned off the projector.

"Now," she said, "I'd like to ask you for a favor."

Margaret took the lead. "Anything, Caroline. My team and I are most appreciative of all the work that you've done with us." Several heads nodded around the table. "You made it possible for us to get our numbers right and show our executives that we were being successful. The dashboards that you've put together for us are making it possible for us to manage our business better. In fact, we're on track for doing over 125% of our quota for this year. So, ask us anything."

Caroline smiled. "Well, this is a big favor. I need you to help me with the manufacturing department. They have some issues with their data and I can't seem to convince them that there are ways to solve their problems. I need you to show them what you've done and how you did it. I think they'll find your story inspirational."

"We'd be glad to help," Margaret said. "In fact, Wally, why don't you schedule a joint meeting with Ed, the VP of Manufacturing, and his team? We'll take them through the data cleanup project, the data stewardship program we put in place and the executive dashboards that we developed. Do you think that will help, Caroline?"

"That would be perfect," Caroline said. "I think with you taking the lead in the meeting, Margaret, they'll also see that executive leadership is very important. Thanks for your help. Now, I also have one more request."

Margaret tilted her head and looked at Caroline. "There's more?"

"Yes. I'd like for you to include in your presentation the changes that you had to make in your organization to keep making progress on these issues."

It's Not Easy

Margaret frowned. The truth was she had not been completely on board with this data quality, data management stuff when Wally had first told her how he hoped to fix the problem between sales and finance, but she had gone along with Wally and Caroline's proposal because they seemed so convinced that it would make a big difference to the business.

It had been hard for her to finance each stage of the project because her own management could not quickly see the return on the investment she was making. She had moved funds around throughout her organization to finance the data cleanup project and then had begged for extra funding to help set up the executive dashboards that were now all the rage in the sales department. She had relied heavily on Caroline's experience and had often consulted her when it seemed that she just couldn't make progress. Finally, Caroline had reminded her that she was changing the culture within the company, not just funding projects.

Margaret remembered the day she had gone to Caroline with her biggest problem. Wally, who managed the sales operations team, was inundated with the data quality projects that he and Caroline had taken on. While Wally was working hard to fix data, the rest of the operations team was floundering. With Wally so engrossed in the data management processes, the team was not performing well. Margaret's monthly report to the VP had been a week late and her own job was now in jeopardy. She had gone to Caroline to tell her that the data projects would either have to be put on hold or managed by IT where they belonged.

"I can't have Wally involved in this project any longer," Margaret had told Caroline that day. "I need him focused on sales ops. I'm hiring ten new reps this quarter and he needs to manage getting them on board and productive. I'm sorry, but we can't afford this project any longer."

"I'm sorry to hear that, Margaret," Caroline had said. "So have you considered all your options?" Caroline pressed Margaret. "I know that Wally is an important part of your operation, but so is the data that you depend on. What would happen if you re-thought completely the way you're organized? Could you manage these projects as part of your business instead of managing them as separate tasks?"

At first, Margaret was irritated by Caroline's questioning. But then she began to think about it. Maybe she could reorganize the sales operations team in a way that would make these data projects part of the team's roles and responsibilities. She had to make these tasks part of the everyday course of business. She had been slightly embarrassed that she had not thought of it herself.

"I think I can do that," she said to Caroline. "But you'll need to help me find the right people to put on the team. Some of the existing team will make the transition well, some won't. Will you help?"

Caroline had been eager to help Margaret with the task of reorganizing sales operations. Margaret's feeling had been justified. Like all change management projects, this one had had its challenges. Three of her sales administrators had quit and one had been given a job in another area. She had given Wally the job as Sales Operations Director and together they had replaced half the team over the last six months.

It had been a difficult, arduous task, but today the team was doing more than just reporting: they were contributing to her business decisions, giving her facts to back up her feelings about her customer base and the market. In the end, it had been worth it. But how could she begin to make the manufacturing vice president understand this.

Margaret turned back to Caroline. "I'll give it a shot. Just tell him that it's not easy," she said, as she picked up her notebook and began walking out of the conference room. "Tell him it's not easy to change the culture."

7

Start at the Top: Putting Data Management on the Executive Agenda

Senior executive sponsorship of the company's overall data initiative is absolutely critical. If you do not get executive support, you will fail. It may be a slow death or a quick one, but it is inevitable. End of discussion. The lack of sponsorship will inevitably translate into insufficient funding for data management programs and delays of necessary business decisions that drive data quality policies. More than any other initiative within your company, data management must be seen by those in charge as being absolutely crucial to the company's success. Garnering executive support is difficult because data management projects are long, expensive, often arduous endeavors that do not produce results immediately.

There are several reasons for the lack of executive sponsorship for data management. Not understanding the complexities of the problem or the resulting consequences of a laissez-faire attitude ranks at the top of the list. Executives can quickly see and trumpet the results of bad data, but often do not attribute it to the lack of business processes associated with the handling of data or with the systems that support those processes. They see these as issues that belong to the IT department and, as such, leave business decisions regarding data management to someone else. In reality, only part of the problem can be addressed by IT. To these executives, it's *just* data—ones and zeroes. IT can handle that. Why is that so hard?

The correlation between data issues and business process is not intuitive and needs to be highlighted and exploited, brought into the open so that executives can begin to understand the implications. When senior executives *are* involved in enterprise data management, it's usually because they've experienced some internal or external crisis that involved data. For example, they've failed a Sarbanes-Oxley audit or they've had a privacy breach. Those kinds of data issues get their attention quickly. Suddenly, the importance of managing data is elevated from an IT issue to a business one. How to accomplish that transition when there isn't a crisis is the purpose of this chapter.

Securing senior executive sponsorship can ensure a sustainable, high-quality data management program in your organization. Securing a senior executive champion can make data a star and, if successful, make the executive a star as well.

Bottom line: A mental model—intuiting a solution because you've done it so many times for so many years—is never as accurate as using data to help with the solution. This doesn't mean to depend totally on data; it simply suggests that decisions supported by data are better decisions than those made purely on past experience or "gut."

But you know that already, you say. So do you also know that the modeling that you do to support a decision is built on your company's data? How good or bad that data is determines the quality of the decision model that you create. Here's an example. Let's suppose that your company categorizes customers by how they are covered by your sales force. Your company grew rapidly and as customers were located and sold, the sales representative who did the finding and selling got the credit for the account. Your ERP system entered the customer into the system using the sales representative's input for the name of the company, the industry it represented and the number of employees that were at the customer location. As your company grew, it became necessary to develop different types of salespeople—those that sold into large accounts and those that sold into smaller ones. Your management even decided to service these two types of customers differently. The large accounts would get face-to-face sales reps calling on them in the traditional manner. Your smaller customers would be supported by an inside telephone sales team. So you set out to segment your customers between those larger and smaller accounts. Easy, right?

The data that you have in your systems can provide this segmentation, but does it accurately reflect the market and will it serve your customers? Take this example through the process. On the first day of deploying your new approach to sales, you discover that 70% of the accounts in your system are small companies, or at least they appear to be. What you discover on looking closer is that over half of that percentage consists of branches or subsidiaries of very large companies. How will that affect your go-to-market strategy? Will you give all the subsidiaries of Beatrice Foods to one account manager or allow each of them to be covered by inside sales at the unique headquarters locations for each subsidiary?

Inherent in this example are process, data and business issues. But at the heart of these issues is the management of the data. Who is allowed to create a customer in your company? Are they required to create customers by using a legal definition of the company? If so, do they match that legal definition against any outside database that will allow you to establish a hierarchy of subsidiaries and headquarters? Is your customer defined for one country and redefined for another? Once the customer is defined, is it also given a unique ID within your systems? Does that ID follow this customer from opportunity to purchase to service? What additional information do you append to that customer record? Who decides what industry this company represents? What additional information do you require in order to segment this customer for sales or service?

Here's a simple test for you. Ask your sales leader how many customers you have. When she tells you, ask her how she defines a customer. Then ask your IT manager the same question. Hopefully, you get the same answer. If you don't, you may have a data management issue around the most important part of your business—your customers.

But why should that matter? It may not unless you want to get into new markets, grow your existing base, or service your customers more efficiently. Here's an example of why it might matter. Let's assume that you want to move your company into a specific vertical market. You've done your research, understand the wants and needs of this market and produced products and price points that should appeal. Since this is an adjacent market space for you, you decide to use your existing customer base as the launch into this market. You rely on your internal data to tell you which industries your customers represent. How confident are you that you know your customers' industry preferences? That wouldn't happen to you, you say. Of course not, but every day executives are making decisions about markets and about spending substantial amounts to capture markets—assuming all the while that data and information is readily available in their in-house systems.

The complexities of data and its correlation to business process and success are not often well understood by senior executives. Senior executives can't spare the time to discuss topics that don't drive their goals, strategies and subsequent stock prices *today*. And often linking those goals and strategies to data and data management is difficult and tedious to explain. Therefore, you must find a way to raise information management to an executive agenda item by linking cause and effect in business terms. Exhibit 7.1 lists some common problems and potential solutions to get management involved.

Exhibit 7.1. Getting Executive Management Attention

Problem	Solution
Unclear link between data and business	Align data program to company strategy
"Data" viewed as "too complex"	Create a data utility function (center of competency)
Data is boring	Collect data "stories." Leverage a data crisis.

Ways to Get Management Attention
Take Advantage of a Data Crisis

Clearly this is not the best way to get attention but it may be the most effective, especially when a natural crisis has not put data management on the executive agenda. When an internal or external crisis occurs that is directly or indirectly caused by "bad data," grab it and make it the case for enterprise data management. Executive sponsorship will come as a result of managing this effectively. Here are some examples of crises that could be linked to data:

- A CEO leaks to shareholders weeks before a quarterly report that the company's revenues will be up significantly over the previous year. Unfortunately, when actual revenue is reported, he has to retract that statement.

- An engineer provides critical customer information to a third-party supplier without the customer's consent. Not a problem until the customer sues and decides to argue the virtues of his case in the press. Although the press may position this as a breach in data privacy, it can be easily linked to the lack of data process management standards and policies.

- The IT department thinks nothing of relocating all the company's highly confidential European customer transaction data from London to China. Then, they discover that to do this rather simple internal move required that they have legal documents in place and that public opinion of such a move could cause negative press coverage.

Crises don't have to be press worthy, however, for executive teams to take special note of them. Sometimes, they just have to be embarrassing. For example, consider this situation that happens more often than database marketers will admit.

You have a special announcement for your largest user event of the year. Invitations have been sent to hundreds of thousands of your best customers. Enrollments are going splendidly and then your customer support line receives a call. One of your best customers has received an invitation addressed to "A******s." (Propriety prohibits the use of the name associated with the unmentionable part of the body.) Stop!

While you're rushing off to uncover the cause of this problem and the culprit who entered the data, remember to evaluate the processes that got you here in the first place and make sure that you communicate to all executives involved (and there will be plenty) exactly how this could have been prevented. Be sure to articulate what it costs in resources and lost opportunity to track down all the points of failure in the process that produced this embarrassment. Tie the prevention to your overall data quality plan and make sure that the executives know what that plan is. In other words, take advantage of the crisis.

If these crises don't happen often enough or aren't visible enough, collect them.

Collect all of them, whether large or small. The more you have, the worse it looks and the better you can take advantage of the problems to present your data quality solution. Although it's not being suggested that you create these crises, should they occur you can use them to your advantage.

Perhaps the single biggest crisis to hit corporate America in recent years has been Sarbanes-Oxley. With the passage of this act, suddenly executives who had never thought about data accuracy or their companies' underlying data infrastructure were forced to consider these important issues. Being on the lookout for these kinds of missteps and then linking them to data quality and management issues can help advance your cause. Other legal compliance issues in the United States and beyond, such as CAN SPAM or the United Kingdom's do-not call list for businesses, may force a crisis as companies attempt to respond to these new laws. Carpe diem! Seize the moment and be ready to link these issues to data and its management.

Link Information Programs to the Overall Company Strategy

One of IBM's key initiatives since 2002 has been e-business on demand. In the past few years this has evolved to "innovation," as in many large technology companies. The company executives are determined to showcase IBM as the leader in these areas not just by telling customers to embrace it, but by driving internal innovation and transformation as well. As a result, IBM developed "information on demand" programs that couple enabling-data capabilities with key e-business-on-demand capabilities.

But what about companies who are not in the high tech business? After all, we all know that data is a technical problem and that high tech companies can solve technical problems more easily. Right?

Driving customer experience is the latest hot topic for CEOs. Positive customer experience leads to more satisfied customers who buy more. David Frankland of Forrester Research cites Harrah's as a prime example of a company that links customer insight to the firm's overall success. In his research paper, *Best Practices: Socializing the Customer Database*, Frankland says: "Harrah's successfully leverages the rich insights within its customer database informing marketing, customer interventions on-site at properties and online interactions." Frankland goes on to make the point that "David Norton, SVP of Relationship Marketing at Harrah's Entertainment, is on the firm's senior executive team."

Once the value of data is understood by management, those who can link that information to the company's overall goals are those who get a seat at the table with senior management. This is how you know you've made the connection.

Make Information a "Utility Service" to the Organization

When beginning a program to bring business information to the organization in a meaningful way, it's often necessary to find and consolidate all the smaller, skunk work programs that operate throughout your company. Undoubtedly, there are those areas of the company that will understand firsthand how and why data management is important. Often those who are involved in paying vendors, sales reps or employees are the first to start data quality programs. If the data at these points in the business process are not pristine, the cries from customers, vendors and employees will get management's attention. Identifying those pockets of data quality management within the company can often serve as a base from which to build a corporatewide initiative.

Once these pockets have been located, you might consider organizing for consistency of approach. This may or may not mean pulling everyone who is involved in data management into one team or organization, but it will require driving consistent approaches and tools from each of these entities and sharing best practices. For example, if the human resources organization has already established a process by which data for names and addresses are matched and managed, why should marketing have to recreate the process? If manufacturing has developed a process for evaluating data as it moves from one system to the next, why should sales adopt a completely different process? Without reorganizing into one data management team, you can begin a data management program that benefits the entire organization.

Another way to drive enterprise data management broadly across a company *is* to consolidate information projects and information assets into one organization and create a "utility service" for the rest of the company (see Exhibit 7.2). Like your phones, recruiting or email service, centralization and consolidation of this function can help drive consistency across the organization and reduce costs as well as provide visibility for data management.

Here are two important considerations before you take this approach. One, don't let this team be dubbed the "Quality" team. Often when quality is pushed to a team to manage, quality becomes *the* responsibility of this team and this team alone. Data management and data quality should belong to everyone in the organization who touches data. Just as product quality is not the sole responsibility of the product development organization, data quality should not become the responsibility of only one team.

Two, moving data management into one team can also mask the complexity of information management to users and executives within the company. Although this is helpful in getting attention to the issue, it can dull the pain for management to such a degree that it no longer deserves their attention. Once it falls off the agenda as something that should be attended to, the data management team and its charter are often considered prime targets for outsourcing. Although outsourcing some of the functions of data management might be the right approach for your company, outsourcing the responsibility for data and information management and usage could mean outsourcing your competitive advantage. It should be core to your company's success.

Exhibit 7.2. Data Utility Function (Center of Excellence)

Function	Example
Centralize data used by all business processes	Customer, product, employee data
Regularly measure and improve data quality	Timeliness, accuracy, completeness, validity
Provide easy access to data	Reports, Web access, dashboard, analytics
Support key company objectives	Revenue growth, cost reduction, re-engineering

Remember, your goal is to ensure that data management is core to your business. For this utility function to be successful and contribute to business success, you must tackle several key tasks:

- **Identify the few, select trusted data sources used by all business processes.** In companies that depend on a sales force, the data used to pay their sales representatives is the best data in the company. In product-oriented, manufacturing companies, the best data might be customer shipping data. At a minimum, consolidate these trusted sources into the utility function.

- **Ensure high-quality data content.** Start by measuring the quality of what you have in place with your trusted data sources. This could entail implementation of a specific program to either protect the data quality of the trusted sources or improve it over time. Either way, ensuring the quality of these sources is paramount. Document the quality of the trusted sources in the enterprise metadata repository.

- **Provide easy access to this data.** One sure way to sink a data quality program before it even gets started is to create barriers to accessing clean, quality data. That's like building a water system to ensure clean drinking water to a community and then not providing the system of pipes to bring it into the home. You have to build a system that supplies your data to its users in an easy-to-use, cost-effective manner. This may also require that you think about how quickly you allow access to this data as well. Real-time access to data could be a requirement for some of your users. Make sure that you understand this requirement fully before implementing systems or processes that turn over data to users instantaneously. Real-time access to data also may carry significant technical performance issues if systems are not architected for this type of access.

- **Align with the company's key initiatives.** From the very first day the organization is announced, make sure that it is aligned with the senior leader's most important goal for that year. If revenue is top of mind, consider boldly declaring that the organization will contribute to some portion of the company goal. Now is not the time to be shy; be bold and go for it! If expense management is a top goal, make sure that you demonstrate ways to save the company money. Analyzing processes and making small changes in data management often produce huge monetary benefits. Make sure that the entire centralized team is focused on the goal. If you show benefits early, your job of creating relevancy for data management will become much easier.

- **Drive standards and policies for your trusted sources across the company.** Without these standards and policies for use and maintenance of your trusted sources, you can't expect to keep these sources clean or ensure appropriate usage. Standards and policies are easy to write, hard to institutionalize. This task is best accomplished with as much collaboration as possible across the company. But collaboration has its price. It requires time. A focused data management team backed by solid standards and policies should be recognized as valuable to the company within 18 to 24 months. Perseverance is the number one attribute of a data management employee.

Senior management commitment is still required in this centralized utility model, but often the size of the organization requires that a senior executive be assigned this responsibility. This alone makes the function worthy of senior management attention. The other advantage of appointing a senior executive to head a centralized organization is that it gives the function a "voice," someone to speak and evangelize the enterprise information issues and benefits across the corporation. Centralizing the competency also provides a visible point of contact in the organization. Centers of excellence are emerging as a key model for enterprise data as data become more central to the corporation.

Set a Big, Audacious Goal

Here are the facts about business today: It's not about what you did last quarter, but what you did today and the greater the number, the better. Executives are number driven and interested in initiatives that help the bottom line. They usually like a little risk and stretch in their goals as well. Whether you're the chief executive or a manager, everyone has a boss they are trying to impress. For CEOs it's their board of directors. They, too, must answer to someone. To be able to get data on their agendas, you may also have to take some risks and set some big, audacious goals that they can see add to their ability to execute better, faster or less expensively.

Exhibit 7.3 gives some examples of goals for data that get attention. Remember that the number you pick for your goal is dependent on your business. Think big and take a risk.

Exhibit 7.3. Attention-grabbing Data Goals

Type of data	Goal
Product install data	Generate $1B by identifying customers whose products are at end of life and who are likely to buy upgrades or new products.
Marketing contact data	Identify 25% more new customers through your Web site
Financial data	Accurately forecast sales for 4 straight quarters
Manufacturing	Maintain a parts forecast accuracy of +/- 5%

Appoint a Senior Executive for Data

One of the quickest ways to get an executive to pay attention to data is to give her responsibility for it. Appointing a senior executive for data highlights the importance of data and provides a single go-to person for all the issues associated with data management. Later we will acquaint you with the role of Chief Data Officer (CDO), the main person responsible for data. However, you don't have to name a CDO in order to shine executive light on the issue of data in your company.

Summary

Putting data quality and data management on the executive agenda is simply a matter of linking facts about how data management can contribute to the company's overall goals to the emotional reasoning of an individual who has the authority and the will to lead in this area. The most important qualities that you must have as you drive toward making data quality and management an "agenda item" is patience and vision. Make sure that you can clearly articulate the "art of the possible," that you believe it and that you can describe it so that others do as well.

8

Managing Data as a Company Asset

Enterprise data management is a corporate program that results in managing your data as a company asset. Managing this asset requires creating comprehensive programs, policies, and metrics. These programs are not unlike those applied to other corporate assets such as people and capital.

LOSING A COMPUTER VS LOSING DATA

Think about the ways your company manages human resources, physical and financial assets. For these, there is no lack of business processes, metrics and policies to acquire, develop, maintain and manage them. Test this theory by losing your laptop computer. Undoubtedly, within hours, you will get a call from someone in your finance department who is responsible for managing this physical asset. He will record the loss of your asset and arrange for a new one. He will also be responsible for reporting the loss of this asset that month on an internal report that goes to your chief financial officer and perhaps. He will record the loss of your asset and arrange for a new one. He will also be responsible for reporting the loss of this asset that month on an internal report that goes to your chief financial officer and perhaps your HR director. If you lose too many laptops in a month, you may trigger an escalation that will launch an investigation.

Now, let's assume that one of your sales representatives leaves the company. On his last day with your firm, he downloads all the company names and associated contacts that he was responsible for during his tenure. What steps does your company take in this situation? Do you even have a way to determine IF this happens? Although not a data quality issue, the point clearly illustrates that data assets need the same rigorous management policies and structure that any asset in your company should have.

Managing data also involves creating roles and responsibilities for managing the asset appropriately and providing an environment and forum for decision-making.

Exhibit 8.1. Steps in Managing Data as an Asset

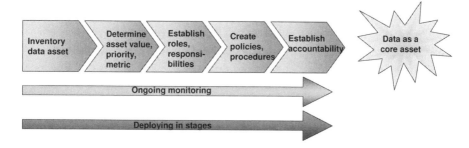

To start, you need an inventory of what you have. Just as if you were responsible for managing real estate or computers, your first task is to make a list or an inventory of your "assets." Data is no different. The only difference might be that the data inventory will be more detailed than a hardware list and perhaps more difficult to obtain. Just as you would record not only the model numbers of the laptop computers in your organization, you would also catalog the types of applications on each. Data inventories, like those of computers, require extensive cataloging of both the "container" (the database) and its "contents" (the data). As you inventory your data assets, much of the information collected should be stored in a central place.

Asset Inventory

A valuable data inventory does the following:

- Identifies all information assets in the company
- Classifies your data assets in a consistent way, using consistent statistics
- Documents key technical and business information about the information asset
- Documents quality characteristics about the information assets
- Stores information asset "facts" in a centralized place

Identifies All Information Assets in Your Company

This means identifying all the "containers" or databases that supply information to your business and then identifying all business applications that create and use data. For example, if you're responsible for HR, then you should know what databases house employee information, benefits, commissions, etc. These are both the strategic databases that are at the heart of your business as well as the not so strategic ones that were built during the era of "client-funded projects." Every company that was founded and has operated in the past decade knows about these "projects." In times of rapid growth during the late 1990s, these projects were popular because they allowed individual business units to create systems that managed the individual business unit concerns or initiatives quickly without the corporate overhead of integration and compliance. The centralized IT organizations often couldn't or wouldn't support projects that the business felt were needed.

The pendulum in that era swung widely to the client side of the client-server world. In today's world, however, the pendulum is making its way back to the more centralized approach with the coming of age of the data center and the ever-present business requirement to reduce cost.

The advent of the Web is also casting an unflattering light on these islands of data. Often Web applications require that all the information you have internally on a customer or business partners be made available through the Web. Where that data resides and how it is managed has confounded thousands of Chief Information Officers (CIO) as they try to streamline supply chain systems with resource planning and marketing systems and bring together all aspects of a customer's interactions with a company. This represents a challenge. First, finding those databases is not always easy. And secondly, once they are found, they may contain pools of important, but often neglected data.

Like all inventory projects, you need a plan that allows you to systematically uncover and document all data sources and data elements in those sources. Your IT department leaders should probably command the project by making available detailed data analyses. In turn, the businesses should then be brought into the inventory process to add their data sources and to alert the IT professionals to the priority and uses of the data that is inventoried. The inventory phase is a perfect time to clean house. Data that is no longer used by the business can be discarded or stored. Consider this phase your "spring cleaning" approach to data management.

Classifies your Data Assets in a Consistent Fashion

Just as if you were classifying laptop computers through model numbers, you will need a consistent view of the data assets that you find. For example, you first have to classify your information assets by whether they originate data, store it or manipulate it. The classification of data assets belongs in the enterprise metadata repository. Following are some examples of these types of information assets.

Originating source data. Originating source data is usually fed directly from an operational system such as order processing or supply receiving. Here the data is created usually by the application designed to manage the business process. Managing data quality at these creation points within a system is tricky and often highly dependent on the data quality checkpoints built into the applications. Since most application designers and software development organizations do not have data quality management backgrounds, this usually means that your applications create "dirty" data.

Here's a real-life example. You have a sales transaction system that is designed to record transactional sales made by your inside sales organization. The sales organization had two important requirements when the system was built: (1) correctly associate with the sales representative who sold the product with the transaction and (2) make sure that the system does not impede sales productivity. With those two, often at odds, requirements in mind, the software developed to manage these sales transactions correctly assigns it to the sales representative, but does not require that the sales agent correctly enter the name, address or phone number of the company. When the system was built, the data management team argued, unsuccessfully, that before a transaction could be entered, the sales representative should do a search on the existing database for a legitimate company name. Because the search added time to the entry of the transaction and caused a perceived impediment to sales productivity, the data management team was overruled. Now, whenever a new company is entered for a sales transaction, "dirty" data is created. Understanding which of your systems are originating source systems is the first classification you should make.

Operational data store (ODS). ODS is a type of database that is used to manage recent information that has to be made available to systems quickly. These databases are usually designed to manage simple queries on small amounts of data. An ODS is a trusted source where data quality and data transformation occur. It can be compared to the RAM in your computer that stores information that is available as long as your system is turned on. In this sense, the ODS operates on information that is updated on a regular basis and could be the system that manages data transformation or calculations. In the last decade, ODS systems were used as reporting repositories for administrative purposes. These are usually the systems that get updated daily, provide business reports, total financial information, or accumulate transactions from various applications. This type system is known as a Class III ODS.

As businesses grew and needed the ODS to perform more complex activities, the Class II ODS came into the IT environment. This type system typically handles more complex information such as sales assignments or product codes and usually is updated frequently—if not hourly, at least daily.

With the advent of Web commerce, the requirement to update systems in real-time or near real-time put more pressure on the ODS and gave rise to the Class I ODS. Then as systems began gathering more and more data from the Web world, the need for another system to interact closer to the data mart or the data warehouse has caused the development of a Class IV ODS. This system is typically designed to help the data warehouse keep its data valid and consistent as it stores more data from more disparate sources.

Master data. Over the last few years, a new type of enterprise operational data store called master data is emerging in many companies. Examples of master data include customers, products, employees and suppliers. A master data store keeps the most critical, commonly used data in each of these data domains and makes this data available to all systems and processes that use it, including the transactional systems, hence the term "master."

Data mart/data warehouse. A data mart or data warehouse contains, for the most part, static data. Just as the name connotes, a data warehouse is a place to "store" your data. This data is typically collected from various sources—both from ODS and from originating systems. Typically, data created in a transactional application will pass through an ODS into a warehouse and/or a mart. But it's not necessary. A data warehouse is usually created either for a particular function or for the whole enterprise. In fact, enterprise data warehouses are very popular and effective. They give a company the ability to pull together in one place all of its data assets. That does, however, require that you have a system for managing data that comes in and goes out of the warehouse—just as if you were managing the distribution of a product. Warehouse data management is a growing part of enterprise businesses and requires a manager with skills unique to this area.

Unstructured data assets. Unstructured data assets exist outside of structured databases, but yet are still critical data sources for the firm. Examples of unstructured data include data stored in spreadsheets, paper documents and on the Web. At a minimum, the asset inventory should list the data contained in the asset, the owner of the data assets and where the data asset is kept.

Managing both structured and unstructured data is important for information security and privacy compliance. We'll delve deeper into this topic later.

Describes Each Information Asset Using the Same Type of Statistics and Language

For example, you might want to describe the databases in your inventory by how many records each has, or how many applications feed the database, or how many reports are generated from each data source. In describing these assets, however, it's very important that you maintain the same definitions as you inventory. For instances, if you are describing your data assets by how many reports are generated from it, you will need to make sure that you clearly articulate what constitutes a report—what it is and is not. Clarity and consistency are the keys to this exercise. These statistics and information about the assets belong in the enterprise metadata repository.

Documents Key Technical and Business Information about Your Information Asset

In this step, you document how the database is constructed. You need to record number of tables, fields and the definitions of each. With legacy systems, this is often the most cumbersome and difficult task. In the late 1990s amid the countdown to January 1, 2000, there were countless CIOs who found themselves trying to catalog legacy systems that had no documentation. This was particularly irksome because they were all trying to find the date fields that could only support formats for 19XX. We would hope that this traumatic, end-of-the world exercise taught them the good practices of documentation and knowledge management, but we can only hope.

These data structures are called "data models." Various data modeling tools can help document the structures of these models. Once documented, this information should be stored in the enterprise metadata repository.

Records Quality Characteristics Such as Completeness, Validity and Freshness of the Data Contained in the Database

Here's the point in your inventory where you can gather some insight into the value of your data assets. Just as you apply value to the products in your product distribution warehouse, you need to apply value to your data. The result of this step should be a report that shows you how complete, valid and timely the data is in each of your database assets. This becomes a baseline against which all your data quality programs can be measured.

This phase is often hampered by the structure of the database itself. If the data source does not record dates for data creation, you may have a challenge in acquiring a reading for timeliness. However, measuring completeness should be simple: Is there data in the field? Yes or no? Measuring validity is a bit more complicated, but just as doable. Here you will need to measure whether the data contained in the field is appropriate. For example, a field for email address is only valid if it is composed of "string@string." This step in the process is equivalent to counting products on the shelves of a retail store. Data quality characteristics should be stored in the enterprise metadata repository as well.

Stores Information Asset "Facts" in a Centralized Place

Unfortunately in most companies, this very critical information, if available at all, is scattered across departments. It not only is decentralized, but often the location of specific aspects of this information, such as who has possession of it, is totally unknown. There are no consistent standards, so the formats used to store the information are usually all different—making its reuse difficult or impossible—and the information is out of date and incomplete. That is where a centralized metadata repository comes in.

The Enterprise Metadata Repository

Metadata is techie speak for "data about data." Practically speaking, the enterprise metadata repository is a catalogue, a digital repository, of all business and technical information and artifacts we SHOULD keep about a company's data assets, including the who, what, when, where, why, and how about individual data sets (e.g., sales department contacts or the marketing department's database of customers and prospects). In short, it's the encyclopedia of all your company's data.

If you're hearing about metadata for the first time, you are not alone. While the technology for metadata repositories has been around for a number of years, most companies have not embraced the enterprise metadata approach to managing their data. As a business manager, the importance of a comprehensive enterprise metadata repository cannot be overstated. The metadata repository is not a geeky technical tool but a critically-important management tool. Yet, the linkages and benefits of a good enterprise metadata strategy are usually not well articulated by the data experts in your company. They present the metadata primarily for its technical benefits, and as a result, you as a business manager may be tempted to view this capability as a "nice to have" documentation exercise or project the team can complete "later" when they have time. Bad decision!!!!! The enterprise metadata repository can be used in many ways that benefit both the business and technical groups, and can be used to solve many of the data problems described in these chapters.

For each information asset in the enterprise metadata repository, the following specific information should be collected:

- Business and technical owner of the information asset
- Data fields in each information asset or the data model
- Physical and logical database layout
- Data definitions for each field
- Data sources
- Timeliness of the data

Allowable values for each data field include:

- Business rules applied to the data , downstream consumers of the information asset, data quality of the information asset
- Special characteristics, such as whether this information asset contains sensitive personal, non-public customer information (PNPI) or company non-public information (NPI)

The enterprise metadata repository can also be used to store more than just data asset inventory and information asset characteristics. The repository should include data governance material such as all data standards, data policies, and authoritative data sources and data control information. This additional information will be very useful to the data leaders in the company as well as the internal and external audit organizations.

Who Should the Enterprise Metadata Owner Be?

Just as Human Resources is the custodian and guardian of employee records for the company and Finance is the guardian of a firm's financial records, a company's enterprise metadata needs one custodian who will serve as its steward. The metadata repository owner will establish the standards—the rules, requirements, and change management processes—that will establish companywide procedures for metadata use.

If a company has a centralized data organization or CDO, the ownership will fall to the head of this organization or the head of technology. Regardless of where in the organization this responsibility lies, the owner should have the institutional power and leadership capability to drive the needed rules and compliance to this very important data asset.

Benefits of Enterprise Metadata Repository

All of the benefits of metadata point to one basic benefit: Greater efficiency. This includes:

- Cost reduction
- Increase in employee productivity
- Faster implementation time
- Better business control

Cost Reduction

Many times managers at all levels of an organization spend a tremendous amount of money reinventing the wheel—recreating data that already exists either in the exact same form or in a similar configuration—because they don't know that it already exists elsewhere in another department. The enterprise metadata repository solves this problem and avoids this cost. Instead of asking the technology team to create a database to solve her "unique business problem," the business manager, with her technology counterpart, first can search the metadata repository to find the information in an existing database. They might also find a database that comes close to providing the information they need and can simply be revised. And of course, the cost of revising information in an already existing database will be less than starting from scratch.

Metadata repositories also lower cost by reducing the overall design and testing time, which ultimately leads to reduced costs of a new solution. Building a new program from scratch involves considerable expense for creation and testing. If all of the existing programs are in one place—the metadata repository—when a new request surfaces, the technologist or the business manger can search for existing programs that reflect the new use. Even when they don't find an exact match and still need a new program, they often find parts of tested and proven programs that can be incorporated directly into the new application. The result is less time (and expense) needed to devote to the new program and less time (and money) needed to test the existing, proven parts of the program—all without sacrificing quality.

Yet another result is the lowered cost of future problems. In the design phase of a new business project, data-quality evaluation and program analysis are time-intensive processes. Oftentimes developers skip this step altogether, causing operational problems later when the program is up and running. However, by using existing, proven data elements, business teams can improve the time and cost of their quality evaluation. Further, by logging these new programs for future reference, they reduce future costs as well.

Increase in Employee Productivity

Business and technical employees waste huge amounts of time searching for information and debating the differences of report results because they used different databases. Consider some basic facts from recent research conducted by IDC [International Data Corporation] in 2001 and then again in 2003:

- The typical knowledge worker spends 15-35%of their time searching
- 50% or less of all searches are successful

A more recent survey was conducted in 2005 by the Center for Media Research and found the following:

- The average worker spends 30% of their time searching
- The cost of productivity lost in searching for data or recreating existing data sources is $18,000 each year per employee
- For typical US corporations there is an average of $5.4B lost hours

While an enterprise metadata repository won't solve all the searching woes of a company, it can solve the unproductive hunting for data. A catalog of all the databases in the company's systems, combined with the additional data-quality information and authoritative source classifications, will tell employees where to go to get the highest quality information. Additionally, by documenting the data terms and data models, employees in the technical community can reuse this documentation to create design documents and test cases.

To encourage all employees' use of the metadata, especially for the non-technical community, a friendly user interface and an effective search tool are important. The enterprise metadata should also be easy to find and access. Consider adding the metadata user interface to your company's home page and publicize its value.

Faster Implementation Time for Business Changes in IT Systems

We've already mentioned that metadata enables business and technical teams to add to an existing database, if possible, rather than recreate new databases to solve their specific business changes. Further, once all databases are cataloged with their quality characteristics and the information is easy to access, the company naturally migrates to using the highest-quality databases. Lower-quality databases can be eliminated or allowed to atrophy on their own. Having fewer databases in the technology landscape creates simplified technical solutions because there are fewer data handoffs from one database to another, fewer data reconsolidations with less data mapping code needed to be developed. This is where the real acceleration of business changes happens. While the metadata by itself does not eliminate the redundant, low-quality databases, it does drive awareness and enables the decisions to eliminate databases.

Better Business Controls—Data Lineage, Data Quality, Data Management

A consolidated view of the data flows of the company's data is now possible with an enterprise metadata repository that contains the sources and downstream consumers (target) of each database in the repository. This "data lineage" can be used to analyze data controls along a data's complete path within the company. Not only will having this data lineage facilitate having the proper controls in place, but will also eliminate duplicate or unnecessary controls introduced because one data process was unaware of the controls of another data process. Both the business controls organization and any business manager who is required to certify a regulatory report will find having the data lineage with the business controls extremely useful in certifying the proper controls have been followed. Additionally, having an enterprise metadata will enable business controls and auditing personnel to go to one place to review the information they need.

Obstacles to Creating an Enterprise Metadata Repository

So why, given all these wonderful benefits, have companies been slow to adopt an enterprise metadata repository? Some companies have tried—and failed—to establish an enterprise metadata program. What are the metadata pitfalls and how do you ensure success of your company's metadata initiative?

Exhibit 8.2. Steps to a Successful Enterprise Metadata

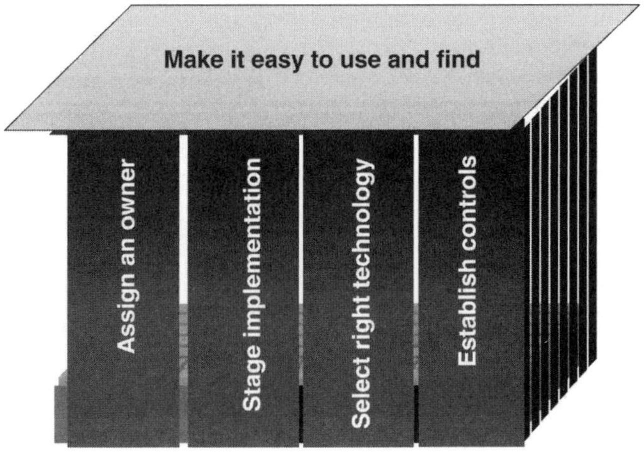

Make it easy to use and find

Assign an owner

Stage implementation

Select right technology

Establish controls

Create the Enterprise Metadata Repository in Stages, by Project, with a Consistent Enterprise Tool, Standards, and Rules

Often, companies embark on a big bang, multi-year, stand-alone project to create the enterprise metadata repository. The business becomes frustrated with the cost and lack of perceived benefits until the project is all done. Don't try to implement an enterprise metadata repository in this way. It will take too long, especially for companies with a large number of databases. Create the metadata in stages and tie it to other large re-engineering projects where there will be obvious data management value to the project.

So why is this approach much different than creating a project-level metadata? Well, in this approach, the metadata implementation will follow common enterprise standards, formats and processes established upfront by the enterprise metadata repository owner. The enterprise metadata repository owner will also select one common technology.

Select a Metadata Technology with an Open, Flexible Architecture from a Technology Vendor with a Committed, Long-Term Investment Strategy

Another inhibitor to a successful enterprise metadata project is selecting the wrong technology. We have previously said the technology has been around for quite some time and several vendors exist. However, each vendor has it owns format for storing the information in their tool, making it difficult to combine all the business, technical information and artifacts a company needs to collect in one product. This is especially challenging if your company is using a packaged software application that has its own database metadata. Vendors are all realizing they need their technology to accept various formats and we suspect in the next five years the metadata technology will get more open and have increased functionality. In selecting a metadata vendor, review their long-term metadata strategy and ensure there is a serious commitment to investing in it.

Just as in other areas of software technology, small boutique vendors are merging with larger software vendors to create a complete suite of information management and business intelligence tools. This consolidation is good for the metadata technology and good for metadata customers as consolidation will create more open, flexible products. Each year Gartner evaluates the vendors and products in business intelligence. As you consider your technology vendor, keep abreast of the Gartner evaluations.

Establish Governance Processes and Compliance Rules to Ensure the Metadata is Kept Current

Another difficulty in implementing an effective enterprise metadata repository is keeping the information current. A stale enterprise metadata defeats all the original purpose of maintaining this level of metadata. Therefore, a critical success factor is keeping the repository current. This is where the owner has to come in again to enforce their institutional power. The most effective way to ensure the metadata stays current is to tie the metadata to a production or operational process. The metadata can also tie to a business control or audit step, like SOX testing.

An ongoing governance board made up of the key metadata stakeholders and the business data stewards should also manage any changes to the rules, processes and formats of the enterprise metadata. The owner should decide what will work for their firm and have the institutional power to report on noncompliance in a regular forum to senior executives.

Invest in Making the Enterprise Metadata Repository Easy to Use, Search and Easy to Access by Your IT Team and the Business Community

Much has been said about the potential for significant productivity and cost improvements across the business and IT communities by having a consolidated repository for all the companies business data. Just as important as the content of the metadata is the accessibility of the information to all who need it. The business and technical teams in your company need to know where to find this information. Once they have, enabling easy searching, retrieving and reusing of the information will ensure the enterprise metadata meets the business goals for data management success. Publicize the business success stories of using the metadata across your company and reward teams when they reuse data versus creating their own databases.

Determining the Data Asset Value

So your data is now inventoried, documented and catalogued in the enterprise metadata repository. Allocating where to spend valuable time and dollars on data management requires prioritizing where to start. That is where determining the data asset value will help. Every asset has a value. And so it is with data. To be treated as a "real" asset, it must be given a quantifiable value. Determining the value of data assets is more difficult than determining the value of capital assets. But it can be done. Assigning a value to all the data the company collects is not practical. Start with the company's most critical data. As noted earlier, critical data is defined as data that materially affects key business objectives, from financial reporting data to competitive advantage data. Customer, product and employee data will likely fall in your critical data list.

Consider the following methodologies:

1. **Customer Data:** Determine the value of your customer data by what it would be worth in an open market. The value could be the price a company would sell its customer list to a direct marketer. Another way to de-

termine the price could be by the value of the acquired customers in a merger with another company. Price could also be set by what it costs to procure a new customer multiplied by the current customer list. The cost to acquire a new customer should be a figure known by the marketing organization.

2. **Product Data:** Use the market capitalization or asset income statement number of your closest competitor to derive a dollar value per the number of products your competitor produces. Then use the value per product of your competitor to multiply by the number of products in your company. If possible, use multiple competitors to determine a range of value/product multiplier.

3. **Employee Data:** Similar to the customer data, employee data could be derived by what it costs to acquire and train a new employee multiplied by the number of employees in the firm.

One other consideration in determining the data asset value is the risk to the firm if the data is released in an unauthorized way. Non-public customer (NPI) information falls in this category. Releasing NPI data carries specific dollar fines. In addition, the loss of the firm's reputation can also be calculated.

Once the data asset is assigned a dollar value other significant dollar metrics are important.

- **Determine the total cost of the data asset, including the life cycle, production and human resource costs.** Why this step, you ask? In doing any inventory in a retail store, your goal is always the same: How much are the goods worth? That becomes your asset. Doing an inventory of your data assets is no different. It can, however, be somewhat more difficult. Isolating each data system and calculating the cost of producing the data, maintaining and managing it will take the combined efforts of your IT, finance and HR departments. The end result should be a total cost of the data assets within your company. And don't be surprised when you find out they are far greater than your cost of goods for products. After all, these data assets are the essence of your business. Exhibits 8.3, 8.4 and 8.5 give you some examples of inventories that could be taken of your different data sources.

- **Working with your CFO, select appropriate return-on-asset metrics.** Examples include:
  —Data quality program cost/number of records in the database. This number would reflect the cost of the insurance policy on your data. Usually this number is small when compared to the total number of records in the database.
  —Data management program cost/company revenue
  —Total cost of data asset /transaction cost

Exhibit 8.3. Sample Database Inventory Record

Database inventory		
	Database A:	Sales opportunity
	Type:	Operational data store
	Record:	200,000
	Owner:	Sales
	Users:	Sales, marketing, customer service
	Data Quality:	Completeness = 99% Accuracy = 80% Validity = 95%
	Business Value:	$10,000,000 replacement cost $100,000,000 opportunity value
	Priority:	High

Exhibit 8.4. Sample Document Inventory Record

Document Inventory		
	Document A:	Customer XYZ, Maintenance Agreement
	Type:	Customer Maintenance Contract
	Owner:	Service
	Users:	Customer service, finance, sales
	Where stored:	Record management system

Exhibit 8.5. Sample Spreadsheet Inventory Record

Spreadsheet Inventory		
	Spreadsheet A:	FAIRVALUE_ASSETS
	Type:	XL Spreadsheet
	Owner:	Accounting
	Users:	Accounting, finance, executive management

So, now you have your data assets inventoried, classified, documented and valued. What next? Now, you need a program to manage or govern these assets in compliance with a world of regulations, policies and procedures. A program to manage your data assets begins with assigning responsibility. And this task should be one to which you give careful consideration. Don't just hand it to the IT management or, for that matter, the CFO. You need to be very thoughtful as to where the responsibility will be managed most effectively and efficiently. True, the majority of CEOs assign this task to IT because many of the processes that must be managed and maintained fall into the technology realm. But more and more leading executives are handing the management of their data over to a new type of leader—a Chief Data Officer. In Chapter 10, we provide a strong case for why you might want to consider just this type of person in your organization.

No matter who gets the job, they will have to develop an asset management program for managing all aspects of your data assets. These include, and are not limited to, organization, policies/procedures and ongoing communications.

Roles and Responsibilities

Let's begin with organization. A good program for managing the Information Professionals associated with data management should include some of the following actions:

- **Inventory the people who manage data in any system in your company.** Assess the tasks that they are performing with the data and identify those that have a sophisticated understanding of the assets that they are managing. In addition to assessing their specific task, map their tasks to jobs identified in Chapter 11 to assess how much of each of these job positions the company has in place. If it's not possible to pool them into one organization, at a minimum create a community of professionals from across the different departments or business units. These people will become your army of data managers, your "knights of the database" who will protect and serve the greater organization. Chances are they've been waiting for someone to come along and lead them for a while. In gathering them into a community, you give credence to work that they may have, at times, thought the company did not appreciate.

- **Define leadership roles.** You've identified those business leaders who are passionate about data. (Don't laugh. They exist.) Now, you need to educate them on what they should understand about data stewardship and how it links to your business. In a subsequent chapter we describe the roles and responsibilities of a Business Data Steward.

- **Develop and grow a core team of business information professionals.** The steps involved in this part of developing your organization are not unique.

They include the steps you would normally go through to ensure that you have a high-performing team. The only trick is to ensure that you clearly articulate what you expect from an information professional responsible for data in your organization. With this in place, you can then evaluate your existing team against your ideal. If there are gaps in education, skills or understanding, you can either hire or outsource the tasks that are required. Only you and your management team can decide how you would need to manage this function. Information management skills will be discussed in more detail in Chapter 11, Get Talent.

Policies and Procedures

Once you have an organization in place that can handle your data assets, your next step is to put in place data management procedures and policies. That's often easier said than actually implemented. If your company has an organization that consults on processes or has instituted Six Sigma actions, then you may find that engaging a Black Belt, a highly trained Six Sigma analyst, to help sort through your data management processes would be helpful.

Six Sigma is a disciplined, data-driven methodology for eliminating defects. The term "Six Sigma" actually refers to the ability of processes to produce output within a specification. In particular, processes which operate with Six Sigma quality produce defect levels below 3.4 defects per one million opportunities. A Six Sigma unit in your organization would have as its goal to improve processes throughout your company to this level of quality or better.

Applying Six Sigma to data management means that you first have to identify all your processes, measure them for defects at various points within the processes and then develop plans for managing those processes to a Six Sigma standard. There are various consulting organizations that can help you with this task if you don't happen to have this capability within your own firm.

Documenting data management procedures and policies is paramount if you want to ensure that your organization manages data effectively. Like all information technology organizations, the data management group needs to ensure that there are policies for acquisition, use and maintenance of your most important assets, like data. These policies and procedures require not only organizational involvement and adherence, but often they require that senior executives endorse them as well. Ensuring that senior management understands the importance of these policies and procedures is the first job of the data management team or the Chief Data Officer. In fact, if possible, it makes a great impact on any organization if the highest officer of the company, the CEO, president or chairman of the board, endorses the company's data management policies. This makes it very clear throughout the corporation how important data is to the company's continued success.

Policies and procedures should address key areas:

1. **Security** refers to both data access and physical security of the data.
2. **Privacy** pertains to the protection of personal identifiable information (PII) that your systems might contain on individuals as well as information that your company feels is non-public.
3. **Storage** means saving your data, archiving it or deleting it when appropriate.
4. **Acquisition** refers to any data that you might purchase to complement, supplement or change your internal records. Acquisition should also cover any procedures for applications that create, read, update or delete data.

Once policies and procedures are in place for these areas, you must make these policies visible across the entire corporation. If your CEO or senior management has endorsed these procedures, then you need only ensure that these policies are visible and uppermost in the thoughts of the management team. Implementing a regular audit program as well as embedding information asset management into other asset management programs often helps with keeping the spotlight on data as an asset. If you can avoid it, don't make your data management asset program a stand-alone program. It should be part of the same audit and management routines that you apply to manufacturing inventories, equipment and real estate. Consider including information management program reviews as part of the existing business control reviews most often implemented by the Finance department.

Asset Management and Accountability

All company assets have asset management processes that ensure they are properly managed. Data assets should be no different. Data assets should be prioritized. Those with the highest revenue value, highest cost or those assets that have the highest risks should be known and managed with strong governance.

Yes, ensuring that the company complies with the standards set forth by your policies and procedures requires *governance.* Compliance to the standards should be mandatory, with exceptions reviewed periodically by senior management. In order to accomplish this, you may need to set up a Data Governance Council within the ranks of your senior management. According to a recent survey of 50+ large companies conducted by IBM, 84% of large businesses believe that poor data governance can reduce the accuracy of business decisions. Good data governance practices, on the other hand, can enable operational efficiencies and regulatory compliance as well as good business decisions.

Data asset management refers to the overall management of usage, costs, availability, usability, integrity and security of data within the enterprise. A sound data asset management program includes a governing body or council, a defined set of procedure, a plan to execute those procedures and an effective set of metrics to ascertain the effectiveness of the programs. In Chapter 10 we discuss the governance forums a Chief Data Officer should consider.

Summary

The initial step in the implementation of a data asset management program involves defining the owners or custodians of the data assets in the enterprise. A policy must be developed that specifies who is accountable for various portions or aspects of the data, including its accuracy, accessibility, consistency, completeness and updating. Processes must be defined concerning how the data is to be stored, archived, backed up, and protected from mishaps, theft, or attack. A set of standards and procedures must be developed that defines how the data is to be used by authorized personnel. Finally, a set of controls and audit procedures must be put into place that ensures ongoing compliance with government regulations.

9

Deploying Enterprise Data Management in Stages

There is no overnight fix for solving all the company's data issues. The enterprise data management program can and should be deployed in stages. Deploying in stages allows for manageable projects to be defined and wins to be demonstrated along the way.

Determining where to start is an important decision to be made by those accountable for fixing the problem. The hierarchy of data needs would have the company start by addressing the safety needs of the firm first. Most companies begin to feel the data pains in this stage and therefore addressing the basic needs first before attempting "self-actualization" is both practical and offers the greatest chance for success. Maslow says that our needs for safety are our most basic human requirements. Your data is no different. The safety needs for data translate into data reliability, consistency, quality, privacy and security.

Although most companies do not report their data pain points publicly, a few statistics have been collected:

33% of companies have failed to bill or collect receivables
33% have been forced to scrap or delay a new system
25% of critical data is inaccurate and incomplete[1]

For those companies that start deploying their enterprise data management program with a data quality program, the benefits can make it worth the trouble. Of those companies surveyed,[2] 75% reported that investments in data quality had positive results. While data-related problems for these companies are often specific, the benefits remain generic:

---

[1] Gartner Strategic Planning assumptions, 2006.
[2] PricewaterhouseCoopers

92

60% cut processing costs
40% boosted sales
50% reported improvement in business benefits

And it's not just managing for today's profitability. Of the executives surveyed, 90% said they expected to increase their use of automated decision-making and other automated processes during the next two years. These increases span the business community, with traditional companies significantly closing the gap on those players who fail to recognize the importance of data. Of those who are still in the dark, one in three said their department data is stored along department lines and not shared across the company. This means that the shift to greater automation will increase these companies' risk exposure to faulty data. A siloed organization does not foster data quality.

Things haven't changed much since the PricewaterhouseCoopers's study that yielded these responses. Organizations that today fail to include data quality analysis and controls in their integration efforts are facing skyrocketing costs for implementation of new systems and rework time for older ones. On the brighter side, organizations that measure data quality at a detailed level achieve more than 50% improvement in business benefits from their data quality initiatives. These statistics give you a reason to start with data reliability, consistency and quality.

Companies that have moved beyond a data quality program and manage their data as a strategic resource are pulling ahead in terms of reputation and profitability from those that fail to do so.

Addressing the Safety Needs of Reliability and Consistency

Chances are that your organization is making or has made a few common mistakes when dealing with data. Here are a few of the things we've heard from data users:

- Our data issues are caused by our systems
- It's easier just to build my own database than to cooperate with an enterprise team
- Over half of our data is old
- We don't need a data architect for this project; it's just a simple system
- Just give me the data this other department used; I'll make it work

So how do you begin to get at the root of these problems? Let's start by being organized in our approach to these challenges.

First, Just Get the Facts

Start with getting numbers associated with the problems described by data users. The conversation between Margaret and the finance manager in Chapter 6 is a perfect example. Many executives *do* know they have data problems. Certain depart-

Exhibit 9.1. Getting at the Root Problems

Problem	Correction
• Too many stories, not enough fact	• Collect objective, measurable facts regularly
• New projects find old data issues	• Joint early planning with business, IT and data experts
• Too many databases, too little quality assurance	• Consolidated, high-quality trusted sources
• Same three repeated data quality issues	• Enterprise data quality program

ments—like Marketing, Research, Compliance and Finance—within for-profit and not-for-profit organizations rely on data in order to make significant decisions that affect their business missions. The very existence of these departments depends on having timely, good-quality data. They are often the biggest advocates for good data and the biggest critics. They complain ferociously about the data problems caused by organizational silos, in particular data-quality issues.

Unfortunately, until a company implements an enterprise data management program, it lacks a systematic, repeatable, objective way—a consistent "data language"—to define problems and develop actionable plans to measure and track data issues and concerns. It is the "urban myth" of "bad data" that drives the companywide perception of the data. Yet when asked to elaborate on the "bad data," only a few specific examples—that do little to define the scope or extent of the problem—are offered up as descriptions of the problem. While an example is useful, it does nothing to help a manager understand if the problem is pervasive or even if this is the most important problem that needs to be fixed in the data at this particular time.

The first thing a business manager needs to know about your data is objective, measurable facts. Business managers have to stop the data "urban myths" by driving reality into the conversations with quantifiable data metrics, a consistent data language, and an aggregated collection of data issues. For example, the conversation between Margaret and the finance manager would change from the "data is bad" to "the sales revenue data has been 20% inaccurate for the last 2 weeks."

Let's understand the process breakdown that caused this discrepancy. In this later conversation, both Margaret and the finance manager understand that this is a pervasive problem, not a single or occasional occurrence. This realization should lead them to conclude that there is a potential, full-scale process breakdown, not merely a one-time technical error. By providing a metric and a tracking mechanism for data issues, the conversation can help define a more actionable problem, narrowing its scope and leading to a speedier resolution.

As a second example, let's use a typical conversation between a product manager and technical administrator of a company's online product catalog. The business product manager is upset at the online catalog administrator because of a problem he saw on the Web today:

"The product price on the online catalog is wrong again!"

A second, more actionable comment would be something like:

"The product catalog did not pick up last night's price change."

The technical administrator would respond with:

"Yes, you're right. My team checked the price change log. The prices were submitted after our agreed-upon change cutoff time."

In this last exchange, both parties now understand that because the price change request was submitted after the agreed-upon cutoff time, it would not appear until the next day.

To prevent this problem from occurring in the future, the business manager must ensure that his team understands the cutoff time requirement and submits the price changes before the deadline. Without logging the time when the change was entered and agreeing to a cutoff time upfront, the conversation was headed in the wrong direction with the technical administrator spending unproductive time chasing a technical error that did not exist.

Both conversations demonstrate the value of having metrics, a common language and a systematic collection of data issues in shaping a more action-oriented and constructive data debate. Plans can now be put in place to address the specific issue and monitor the progress with clear, objective metrics. Apply this time-tested adage to the problem:

> **You can't manage what you cannot, or do not, measure.**

Second, Make Sure that Every New System You Implement Looks at Data As Well As Application Architecture

A different kind of data quality problem occurs during the development of new technology solutions. Data-related problems often surface late in the implementation phase of complex applications, causing data to become unreliable and inconsistent. When they do, they can lead to unplanned delays, additional costs, and endless finger-pointing at those unlucky enough to be responsible for the implementation. Often these "data issues" surface because underlying process and business gaps have not been addressed. Sometimes these gaps are as simple as differing definitions for

Exhibit 9.2. New Project Design Process

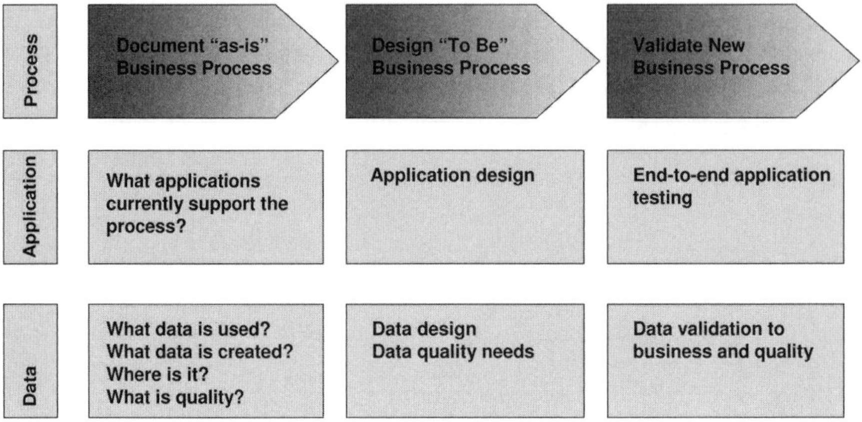

Process	Document "as-is" Business Process	Design "To Be" Business Process	Validate New Business Process
Application	What applications currently support the process?	Application design	End-to-end application testing
Data	What data is used? What data is created? Where is it? What is quality?	Data design Data quality needs	Data validation to business and quality

the same data element. For example, sales has adopted a definition of "customer" that means any company that has been allocated a sales resource, regardless of whether they have purchased or not. Marketing, on the other hand, calls a "customer" any company that has purchased in the past five years. When the company decides to create a system that connects marketing-generated leads to sales, this definition may create problems. By having different definitions of the same data element, sales and marketing may find that their systems don't actually speak the same language. So "data" becomes the issue in this new application.

One way these processes and business gaps occur is by not allocating enough time for proper due diligence in the development of a new business solution. Too many application teams are measured on meeting their project deadlines, not on effective solution implementation. Successful implementers effectively plan, which means allocating sufficient time to tasks related to the business process, application, and data changes, such as:

- Analyzing the "as-is" (current situation) and the "to-be" (new application) business process
- Validating that the application design supports the new process
- Understanding the data requirements of the new process and where the data will be sourced from
- Evaluating the current state of the data against the quality required to execute the process effectively
- Finally, validating that the new process supports the overall business objectives

Unfortunately, some of these steps are often skipped to ensure the implementation deadline date. These steps take time and require a collaborative, iterative approach with all the experts—business, process, data, and application design. Often,

Exhibit 9.3. Data and Re-engineering Programs

		ERP	CRM	SCM	Web Commerce	Operations
	Re-engineering Programs					
Data Used	Customer Contact	✓	✓	✓	✓	
	Customer Sales	✓	✓		✓	✓
	Customer Inventory	✓	✓		✓	
	Customer Order	✓	✓	✓	✓	
	Marketing	✓	✓		✓	
	Supplier	✓		✓		
	Accounting & Finance	✓		✓	✓	✓
	Product & Price	✓	✓			
	Customer Support, Maintenance	✓	✓	✓	✓	
	Payroll	✓		✓	✓	✓
	Manufacturing	✓				
	Commission	✓	✓			

the required players in the analysis and evaluative process—like the business experts—rarely understand why they have to be so involved in all these steps. As a result, they don't invest enough time in evaluating the data requirements in the analysis stage of the development. To keep the project on schedule the technical experts, who lack the business experience, are often left to make critical decisions about how the application should work and what data should be collected, transformed and managed. The result: an application that does not manage the data effectively for the business.

Re-engineering projects that integrate multiple business processes often unearth hidden data problems. Initiatives that integrate business processes and their corresponding information technology systems currently are prevalent trends in most industries. Companies are integrating their businesses to respond to the real-time needs of their customers, to automate their customers' experiences, and to reduce costs. But integrating processes and technology systems without the parallel integration of the data is a formula for failure. Data *is* the common language used by processes and systems to communicate.

Data problems may not surface when you implement one application because its data is self-contained. All data described for that one application works just fine. But put two applications or business processes together, as is the very goal of ERP, CRM, and SCM, and suddenly you find you have an issue. Many companies fall into the trap of thinking their data will work just fine because the data for a particular solution has been individually scoped, defined, and tested. "Of course," the logic goes, "data will be fine when we combine it with another system." That could not be

Exhibit 9.4. How Inconsistent Data Results in Confusion

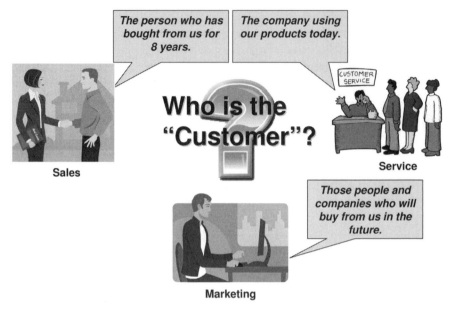

further from the truth, especially if integrating various vendor off-the-shelf solutions. Data issues surface in the integration steps, in the "handoffs" when data flows from one system (CRM) to another (ERP). Circumventing the data analysis prescribed for these steps is practically the same as not equipping the Titanic with enough lifeboats.

So, what could go wrong? Here are some examples of what can happen when data management and quality haven't been considered before implementation.

Data Inconsistency

- Customer name in the CRM application refers to the contact that buys from the sales representative; customer name in the ERP application refers to the company where the product is shipped.
- Address fields in address field in CRM are connected to contact; address fields in ERP are connected to a location for shipping and billing purposes.
- "Order status progression" means different things to different third-party distribution carriers.
- Sales revenue can be booked as "sold" when a product is shipped to a warehouse or to a distributor or installed at a customer or invoiced to a customer.

Data Processing Mismatches

- SCM organization has adopted data standards that are in line with their suppliers; ERP has data standards that conflict, but support the standards imposed by the company's general ledger application.

- Opportunity management system within the CRM application requires the entry of a customer name and address to complete a record. Web applications need only an email address to complete a record, but your applications need to talk to one another.
- Archive data policy for one country's order inventory application is different than for another country's application carrying the same type of information. Doing cross-country reporting comparing past time periods will be tricky.
- When displaying customer order status fulfilled by a business partner, different business partners stipulate how and what status can be displayed. Contracts may require that order status information be displayed per the contract terms and not in a manner consistent with the way the end customer would like to see the data—especially if the customer can check his orders online.
- ERP applications don't require a sales opportunity number to process an order, only an order number. CRM business managers, however, want to trace a sales opportunity all the way from the beginning of the sales process to final invoice. Negotiations will need to occur to ensure this number is passed from the CRM system to the ERP system and kept in the ERP records.

Confusion

Data that is passed between applications and transformed in the process can result in confusion. For example:

- Products and services in the CRM application are associated and given a solutions number then passed to the ERP system that doesn't understand solutions numbers, only part numbers.
- Data stored in a data warehouse is moved into a data mart for providing sales results, but because only part of the customer record is moved, only part of the information can be analyzed.
- Consumer loan or credit card application data is manually reentered from one system to another in order to comply with the company's unique systems requirements. Manual reentry will introduce data errors.

Third, Create a Few, High-quality Databases for Broad Company Use.

Even if your company is not embarking on a large re-engineering project, hidden data problems also surface when there are a large number of databases, with similar data, scattered across the company. Companies that have not managed their databases in an organized way feel the consequences immediately. During business performance reviews and sales management meetings, they waste all sorts of valuable time debating the validity of the numbers or synchronizing numbers across different groups rather than solving problems. Data issues include:

- Databases that have been implemented without an overriding company data strategy cause the same data to be replicated in many places. Compounding the problem, each database collects the same data at different times, creating an "out of sync" condition.

- There is no one place to go to understand the complete inventory of databases in the company. Data users are constantly struggling to find the right database to use to solve their problem. Much time is wasted looking and analyzing databases. Many times the data users become frustrated in the search and resort to creating a new database—yet another repository of information that must one day be integrated.

- Dollars are spent repeatedly to clean the same data, using different business rules to determine "good enough" data.

- Multiple departments across the company procure the same data from the same vendors (such as Bloomberg, D & B). Each department has its own contract with the vendor, with different terms, fees, and usage rights.

Fourth, Add Data Management Activities to Your Critical Business Processes

In addition to the problems created by multiple databases with varying levels of data quality for the same data, most legacy and current applications, as well as business processes, do a poor job of checking for data quality. This is especially true when the data is first entered into the company system. For example:

- Back office data quality remediation has been the norm in most companies for years. How many people do you have assigned to check sales orders, customer Web registrations? How many reports do you have that represent the same views of data simply because you want to ensure that you have the right numbers?

- Most application user interfaces have not been designed to allow for easy entering of high quality data. Legacy systems often have open-ended text boxes, instead of pull-down menu choices. Some legacy systems have limited character restrictions on input fields or, even worse, require special, unintuitive input codes because of limitations in the applications.

- Bad data is propagated to multiple places and cleaned multiple times using different data quality rules. So who or what determines where the highest quality data resides?

If your company is not properly managing the data created and stored inside the enterprise, chances are that the data coming from outside the company is more uncontrolled. As mentioned previously, external data procured multiple times from the same service providers can create issues of data quality, as can transactional data supplied by your business partners, value-add remarketers, dealers, or even your own customers. Most of these relationships, especially those with data providers, are usually maintained by a business department manager and further substantiated with a contract. Yet, it is unlikely that the contract contains any data quality expectations. And even if there are provisions, they are rarely monitored. If monitored, violations are not enforced for fear of alienating the relationship with the partner, customer, or provider. External data often only compounds your internal data problems.

Addressing Data Quality

What is Data Quality?

The short definition of data quality is: It is whatever you believe it to be. Like beauty, it's in the eye of the beholder. Or, more accurately, it's whatever you need it to be. If you're a finance manager, data quality means that you can accurately represent your firm's revenues and expenses in line with standard accounting rules. If you're a sales manager, you might view data quality as an accurate representation of the amount of opportunity you have in the sales pipeline at any given time. If you're a marketing manager it might be the accurate representation of customers and prospects with all names, addresses, company identities verified and accurate so that contacting those customers will be fast and easy.

Exhibit 9.5. Examples of "Good" Data Quality

Business Function	"Good" Data Quality Accurately Represents
Finance	Company revenue and expenses in a financial statement
Sales	Customer account and sales opportunities in a sales pipeline
Marketing	Market opportunity and individual decision makers within identified companies
Supply Chain	Product availability
Procurement	Vendor purchase orders

Because data quality means different things to each part of the business, different data-quality requirements result for the same data. So, to go back to crafting a definition: In order to be defined as "quality," the data must match the reality of that part of the business that is creating, using, and managing it.

Let's start with the part of your business responsible for creating data. Ask yourself these simple questions:

- For application X, who in my organization is responsible for data input?
- Is this person closest to the source of the data? For example, a sales rep might have the most accurate view of your customer's revenues and growth for last year. But does the rep actually input that piece of data into your CRM application? Or does someone in marketing get sales revenue information from a company's annual report?
- What is the best source of information? Are there other sources? Better sources?
- Who is the best person to provide the data?

The issue here is not only who is closest to the source of the data, but who is ultimately responsible for ensuring that the data entered most accurately represents reality. These could be two different individuals or processes.

Getting the answers to these questions means taking time and paying attention to each piece of data in your application. That's why a team developing a new application should include a data architect and someone from the business side (i.e., the user side, such as marketing or sales) who understands the nuances of the data that will be used and managed. This collaboration of data, application development, and business user insight can be the most important distinction between a successful application implementation and a failure. It ultimately makes the difference also between quality data and data that requires extensive upkeep.

The magnitude of the data quality issues you face may vary because of how that data is used. For example, quality of company account information may be good enough for campaign targeting where an address error may result only in returned mail. A far more serious consequence of inaccurate account data, for example, is that the credit rating for an account is mismatched to the account and your company suffers losses incurred from bad debt.

Understanding how the same data is used across the different business functions and what the current view of quality is will determine how much effort you will need to ensure that you maintain the desired level of quality.

Exhibit 9.6 provides a list of different departments and the kinds of data quality that may affect each.

Exhibit 9.6. Key Data Elements by Department

Department	Important Data Elements That Require Accuracy
Finance	Product bookings
Product Development	Product identification numbers
Shipping and Receiving	Stocking unit numbers Customer shipping address
Manufacturing	Product units
Marketing	Customer name, address, title Customer interests Sales representative assigned
Service	Customer satisfaction Customer phone number
Sales	Customer satisfaction Products installed at customer site Sales representative assigned

Three Myths of Data Quality
Quality Issues Are Technical Issues

We have already given a few examples demonstrating how data problems can be erroneously blamed on the technical or IT department. Yet, upon inspection, these problems turned out *not* to be technology related at all. While data quality can certainly be caused by a bad technical design, a programming error or a hardware error, more often the really significant data-quality issues are the result of incomplete or poor business processes and require business leadership to solve. In the example of the product prices erroneously posted to the Web, the product manager implemented business process changes to ensure that all the necessary steps and approvals for price changes were completed before the deadline required by IT. Additionally, staff training was implemented. Both of these changes resulted in on-time price changes.

If your company uses business partners or value-added remarketers (VARs) to provide additional services to your customer, you probably still want to keep accurate account, contact, and transaction information in your systems. Unfortunately, your business partner is not equally motivated to update your system. Fearful of losing the primary relationship with the customer by sharing the precious customer information, they work to share with you only that information needed to complete orders and ship products. They want to own and manage the primary customer relationship. You won't overcome this problem—getting complete customer information—with a technical solution. You will need to change the business relationship to provide incentives or penalties in the contract to ensure that the VAR provides complete customer data.

Still not convinced? Let's look at one more example. It's common for Marketing and Sales to have different data-quality priorities for the same customer data. This leads to conflict in the customer database requirements. Marketing considers the customer data "incomplete" if the job title and job responsibilities of a contact are not included as part of the contact data. This information makes it possible for Marketing to better target customers. Marketing, therefore, wants job title and job responsibility included as a mandatory data field that must be entered by the sales rep when a contact is created in the CRM system. Sales reps know their contacts personally and don't need this information to complete a sale or manage the relationship. They further argue that adding and maintaining this information in the database takes too much time and reduces sales productivity, which results in lower company revenue.

Sound familiar? How does this "data completeness" quality issue get resolved? They don't get resolved with a technical solution. The heads of Marketing and of Sales have to sit in a meeting, brokered by the Chief Data Officer or Chief Operating Officer, and figure out the metrics. By evaluating the quantifiable business value and impacts of both sides of the argument, they can reach a joint decision about whether job title and job responsibility become mandatory fields in the customer data that must be entered and maintained by the sales rep.

We Cleaned the Data During Initial Project Deployment, so It Must Still Be Good

We hate to be the ones to break it to you, *but* data quality is a program that has no end—unless of course, having high-quality, current data is not a requirement for the business process. All data decays. Some believe the shelf life is only two to six months and, therefore, data quality requires an ongoing investment of dollars and people, similar to the organization's investment in product quality and customer support. Look at your own personal business card. What piece of information has changed in the last six months? Did you change jobs and titles? Did you get married? Change your name? Change companies and offices? Move to another location inside the same company? Delete your fax number and add your mobile phone? The list is near endless.

Data quality also degrades because of other issues. For example, the number of people who touch data increases the number of opportunities for defects. If your applications allow incomplete entries or don't check for valid entries, then data quality suffers. In addition, the quality and frequency of the training provided to the data entry personnel also becomes a factor in data quality. People who don't understand what data should be entered can't be held responsible for data that is incomplete or invalid.

The cost and benefits of data-quality investments must be measured yearly to ensure a positive return on investment. Appropriate investments in outsourcing, automation, and tools can drive down costs just as you would expect to do with any other ongoing maintenance expense.

"Good Data Quality" Means the Same Thing to Everyone

Like art, data quality is in the eye of the beholder or, in this case, the user of the business process that uses the data. The previous example where Marketing's definition of "good data" included the job title and job description yet Sales did not, demonstrates this myth well. The details of the customer order data required by Sales and Marketing is different from the customer order data required by Manufacturing to build the order. A much more detailed bill of materials is required for the customer order data to be "good" for Manufacturing. Many data disasters have occurred when one group assumes the data used by another process will work fine for their process. "Just give me their data" has been said many times—with very little success. Do the proper diligence to ensure the data fits your process.

Who is Responsible for Data Quality?

If data quality belongs to anyone in a company, chances are that the IT department has been tagged. If that's the case in your firm, then IT is probably managing it as an IT asset. So, what does that mean to the welfare of the business? It means that someone will watch carefully to ensure that the data is "accurate" and relevant to the business operation so that all systems work appropriately and data doesn't stop a process.

But managing the content or accuracy of the data may still fall to the business. If this is the case in your organization, you will need to know how to manage data as an enterprise business asset with the same disciplined attention that managing other assets requires.

When data is relegated to an IT responsibility, the business side (the user side) may lose its influence on data quality. Despite this challenge, most companies relegate this function to IT. A recent Gartner Group survey reported that the majority of the respondents indicated that IT had sole or near-sole responsibility for data quality (see Exhibit 9.7).

Exhibit 9.7. Parties Responsible for Data Quality

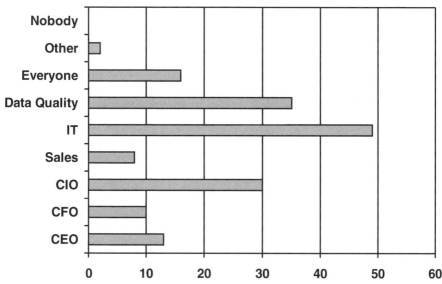

Source: *Gartner Research, Garnter Study on Data Quality Shows that IT Bears the Burden, February 23, 2006.*

If IT is accountable for the quality of your data, then the business operations must be actively drawn into the process because they own applications or systems of record that generate the data. This is not just a matter of "IT against the World" (i.e., the rest of the company). For example, whose responsibility should it be to manage customer data that is input by the accounts receivable department—IT or Finance?

Here's a good test to answer that question: Begin at the source. If the accounts receivable clerk is responsible for data input, then the responsibility lies with accounts receivable. In this instance, that department should drive the processes for quality entry of the data. If data use and flow between and among different applications are addressed during the program development phase, data-quality problems are minimized and made more manageable further down the road. Too often the department responsible for data input doesn't understand its role in creating quality data and managing that quality.

Let's assume that clerks must enter the name of the company into the accounts receivable application. How does the clerk get the right name? Does the application allow for search of possible alternative names or does it require that the clerk use his or her judgment? This often means that simple company names such as IBM get reflected in the system in the following ways:

- International Business Machines
- International Business Machines, Inc.
- I.B.M.
- IBM

The legal name for the company is International Business Machines, Inc. Although the accounts receivable department may not care about the proper spelling of the company name, downstream applications might. For example, the accounts receivable may carry "IBM" and the shipping department might have "I.B.M." as part of the data they maintain. This doesn't matter unless it's important that the shipping department application talks to accounts receivable. If you can't match the two IBMs in the system, then you may not be able to collect your money for the product that you ship.

Here's where the IT department comes in. IT is often enlisted to help take data output from one business process and input it into another. To do this, IT usually has to perform what is called ETL (extract, transform, and load). This process makes it possible to move data accurately from business application to business user.

How Do You Manage Data Quality?

Dun & Bradstreet, the largest provider of business-to-business data in the world, knows just how fragile the quality of data can be. The company estimates that business data decays at an average rate of 2% to 2.5% per month. Here's how D&B depicts it:

In the next 60 minutes in the United States:

- 251 businesses will have a suit, lien, or judgment filed against them
- 246 business telephone numbers will change or be disconnected
- 58 business addresses will change
- 81 directorship (CEO, CFO, etc.) changes will occur
- 41 new businesses will open their doors
- 11 companies will change their names
- 7 businesses will file for bankruptcy

So, in a year:

- 21% of CEOs will change
- 20% of all addresses will change
- 18% of telephone numbers will change
- 17% of business names will change

Obviously, data is extremely fragile. But consider, in light of the D&B insights, the data from your own internal operations, which might manage as many as 10,000 transactions or interactions a day. Each of those transactions is an opportunity to either improve or degrade your data quality.

OK, so let's say that you're one of the few executives who is happy with your internal data quality. But what about the quality of data provided by outside sources, such as suppliers (e.g., list brokers) or another department or division of your own company? No matter which situation exists (and there are multiple possibilities), data coming from an application where the data quality is undesirable (we'll come back to the notion of "bad" in a moment) will contaminate your "perfect" data. Any of these situations can—and do—produce charges of "bad data."

And in every-day situations, "bad data" can be a showstopper. When it stops the show depends on the application development or implementation processes being used and how much time and attention are given to the design of the data architecture before an application is built.

So managing data quality comes down to managing all contributors to poor data quality. This includes the process, people and technology items listed in Exhibit 9.8.

What Actions Should You Take to Ensure Ongoing Data Quality?

It's this simple: Invest and commit. Invest your time, your people and your funds.

First, maintaining quality data is a collaborative process. Invest in a collaborative data design process that involves members from IT and the business side of the company who are active in every application development project that you attempt. Ensure that everyone who touches the data has a part in the decision about its quality. This can help you not only with issues such as funding, but can also help you evangelize the need for data quality.

Second, formally appoint people to manage data quality. These are often called data stewards, and we'll discuss their role later in the book. People appointed as stewards should understand not only the business processes that use the data, but how the data is managed by and through the various business processes.

Third, ensure that you set aside sufficient funding to maintain the data in each of your department's or company's business processes. The specific amount depends heavily on your starting point. Do you have years of neglect to manage through or have you managed your data well and just need a slight tune-up?

Wherever you start, remember that you are embarking on a long-term, never-ending process. It should get easier, but it will always be a necessity.

Where Should You Start a Data-quality Program?

Where to start a data-quality program depends on where you are. You need to understand what data is affecting what part of your business the most. Just because your sales force says that their customer data is "bad" doesn't mean that correcting the customer data that they see in their CRM application is the first place to start. Start with the place in your business where: (1) the data quality can be measured—no matter how simply, (2) there is a business process that can be articulated and is well understood, (3) someone within your organization is willing to assume responsibility for a data quality project and (4) you feel comfortable supporting a project that may not show value for a few quarters or a few years.

For example, let's assume that you select a project in your manufacturing division. Your processes are well understood and initial evaluations have shown that your supply chain data does not conform to a set of standard values. Because of this,

Exhibit 9.8. Contributors to Data Quality Problems

you are seeing higher-than-industry averages for overstocking costs for similar but slightly different products. This is also affecting the volume discounts that you give to your vendors and your costs for restocking are growing. These may all be symptoms of a lack of data quality, but they may appear, at first, as business process or performance issues.

Getting to the heart of what causes a performance problem often leads you to data quality. In fact, one industry study estimates that the total cost of data quality to the US economy is over $600 billion per annum.[3] Today, there are countless organizations and consulting firms designed to help you manage data quality projects. Here are the kinds programs you might use to get to the heart of your data issues:

- **Data profiling or assessment.** This type of project is usually the first a consulting firm will recommend and is designed to give you a view of your data and the areas where it can be improved.

- **Data standardization.** Often this project is designed to help you establish rules that ensure that your data conforms to certain standards. These can be specific to your business or defined by your industry.

- **Address standardization.** A few companies specialize in ensuring that name and address data within your systems are maintained against US and worldwide standards.

- **Matching.** This process may be employed to help you compare records from one system to another. Often information in one system may not have a natural link to information in another. If that happens, you may need to match against common elements in both records. This is often done with name, address and/or phone number. Matching may be strict or loose depending on the application. For example, you may want to be very strict with your matching of tax ID numbers from one record to another, but you might want to be looser in matching "Jim" to "James" in a contact record where the Jim's address matches James's.

- **Linking.** Linking projects often involve matching records first and then linking them together. The result of this process often results in a richer data record. For example, a record for ABC Company that contains its product purchases might be linked to records in your CRM system to give you a more accurate picture of the different departments within ABC that are purchasing your products.

- **Monitoring.** Consultants doing these kinds of projects often first perform data assessments then continue to monitor your data to ensure that the

---

[3] *The Data Warehousing Institute Report Series: Data quality and the bottom line* by W. Eckerson, 2002.

processes they put in place maintain a prescribed level of quality. These firms may also offer ongoing maintenance of your data as a service.

Addressing Privacy and Security

Addressing privacy and security needs for your data begins with support from the business leaders. They play a critical role in establishing the classification for the business value of the data and determining what data should be protected, where that data is stored and used, and what kind of controls should be used to manage it.

What Data Should be Protected?

Although the value and classification of the data is often determined at the corporate level by legal or corporate data organizations, business leaders are integral to managing privacy and security. Common information security labels used by the business sector to classify internal data are public, sensitive, private, and confidential. Common information security classification labels used by government include unclassified, sensitive but unclassified, confidential, secret, top secret. For example, classifying what is sensitive personal information is determined by the legal department, with direct influence by the laws of the state or country in which the company operates. Classifying data attributes which substantially contribute to a company's financial reporting is done by the corporate data organization or the Chief Financial Officer.

Defining the high-level data attributes that constitute personal or sensitive information protected by legislation can usually be accomplished by the legal or privacy department of your company. These individuals look at industry standards and legal precedence when identifying the attributes. Often, it is not one attribute alone but several attributes used in combination that must be protected. For example, non-public information, or NPI, is the combination of attributes that can lead to identity fraud such as social security number *and* name. The legal or privacy department then turns to the business line departments to do the next level of detailed evaluation. For companies with business data stewards (more in the next chapter) , the job is handed to them. It is up to the business data steward to interpret the high-level attributes into the logical and physical names of the data attributes they manage. This is where having documented data models in an enterprise metadata repository comes in very handy. If this is not the case, then the steward needs to commission the detailed work of identifying the logical and physical attributes, working closely with the application owners. The resulting information should then be stored in the enterprise metadata repository for future use.

Where is This Data Stored and Used?

Once the business value is decided, the enterprise metadata repository should be used to store the classification along with the other descriptive information about the data. Then, the organization can turn to establishing the standards, policies and system checks required to ensure the proper handling, labeling, duplicating, distributing, storing and disposing of critical data. Selecting reasonable and appropriate controls is a challenge. Administrative, logical and physical controls are all types of controls that can be implemented. Controls should be defendable to an auditor or a regulatory body. Equally important, the controls should be reasonable and provide value to the firm in identifying and mitigating the risks of an information security breach. Many companies "gold plate" their controls to ensure all risks are mitigated, but at a very high cost to the company. The business data steward can help provide the proper business judgment to design controls that ensure a balance is reached.

Because of the increasing legislation and risks of information security, most companies have created a corporate information security or a privacy organization, separate from the corporate data organization. The information security organization may have a dedicated staff focused on staying current on the latest legislations in information security and understanding the sophisticated approaches to security breaches. It also sets the information security policies and standards consistent with legal, regulatory and industry standards.

The information security organization partners with the business data steward and the corporate data organizations to leverage the tools (i.e., the enterprise metadata repository) and the data management programs used to manage the structured business data in databases. The information security organization also ensures all company employees and business executives understand their responsibility in protecting the firm's data and in preventing data loss and inadvertent disclosure.

Now the business data steward must find all the databases in her domain that contain these data attributes. Again having all databases documented in an enterprise metadata repository expedites the task. If all databases are not documented, then the business data steward can use the requirement for data privacy management as an "opportunity project" that facilitates getting this information collected and stored in the metadata for future use. If the data is spread in many databases, your steward may need to make the case to consolidate your sensitive information into one database to simplify access and control the costs required to secure this information properly. This is one of the reasons Customer Master Data management is becoming a key investment area in information projects.

What Controls Should be Used to Manage This Data?

The information security organization works with the IT organization to implement the proper security software that can prevent the unauthorized access, change, distribution or storing of information. Software solutions often used to provide security include:

- Firewalls
- Encryption
- Email monitoring

- Security logging and monitoring
- Access management
- Data archiving
- Incident management

While the data governed by information security policies and standards are generally of much broader scope than those governed by the business data steward, the roles of the information security officer and the data steward are converging. The policies covered by information security usually include documents, emails and Web content, the data management processes, practices and roles. Oftentimes the data steward has similar responsibilities.

Controlling the daily access, distribution and archiving of sensitive data is the next level of data management. Fortunately, there are software solutions available in the market today, such as encryption, access management and data archiving solutions. These solutions are also used to manage overall information security.

An interesting data management challenge may be how to store and use sensitive information across the company for testing purposes. During testing of new software solutions, production data is required for parts of the testing process. Using production data that contains sensitive customer records poses a high risk to your company because the data can be distributed and copied more easily than in a protected production environment. Yet using production data is necessary to verify if an application works as designed. Fortunately, there is an answer. Solutions now exist that mask the sensitive data so that it is still valid data, but not the true customer record.

Ensuring the accuracy and completeness of customer information is another data management implication. If customers "opt in" to collecting and storing their personal information and allowing for the use of this information, they can rightly expect the data they provide to be stored and distributed correctly. An ongoing data quality program ensures this happens. Again, having a comprehensive data quality program for customer data has broad benefits across the company, not the least of which is data privacy management.

Summary

To address the needs of reliability, consistency, quality, privacy and security requires that you start with the basic facts about your data situation. Data reliability and consistency can be helped or hindered by the processes you employ in developing applications. Understanding these processes and embedding good quality data management into them can help. Data quality is a process as well that needs to be managed through the community of data stewards responsible for the data supporting their business applications. And lastly, data privacy and security require not only business process support, but must also adhere to government regulations as

Exhibit 9.9. Roles and Responsibilities Matrix

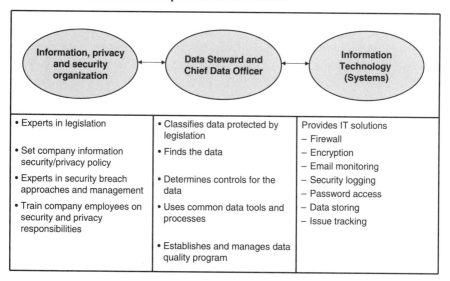

Information, privacy and security organization	Data Steward and Chief Data Officer	Information Technology (Systems)
• Experts in legislation	• Classifies data protected by legislation	Provides IT solutions
		– Firewall
• Set company information security/privacy policy	• Finds the data	– Encryption
		– Email monitoring
• Experts in security breach approaches and management	• Determines controls for the data	– Security logging
		– Password access
• Train company employees on security and privacy responsibilities	• Uses common data tools and processes	– Data storing
		– Issue tracking
	• Establishes and manages data quality program	

well. Ensuring that your data management organization supports all of these basic data needs is essential to the success of your data organization and your business.

For Further Reading

Eckerson, W. 2002. The Data Warehousing Institute Special Report Series: Data quality and the bottom line."

Kahn, B.; Strong, D.; Wang, R. 2002. "Information Quality Benchmarks: Product and Service Performance," Communications of the ACM, April 2002. pp. 184–192.

Price, R. and Shanks, G. 2004. A Semiotic Information Quality Framework, Proc. IFIP International Conference on Decision Support Systems (DSS2004): Decision Support in an Uncertain and Complex World, Prato.

Redman, T. C. 2004. Data: An Unfolding Quality Disaster.

Wand, Y. and Wang, R. 1996. "Anchoring Data Quality Dimensions in Ontological Foundations," Communications of the ACM, November 1996, pp. 86–95.

Wang, R., Kon, H. & Madnick, S. 1993 Data Quality Requirements Analysis and Modelling, Ninth International Conference of Data Engineering, Vienna, Austria.

10

Establishing Accountability and Governance

Appointing a Data Leader

There is a growing trend in companies to expand the CXX job titles beyond the traditional Chief Executive Officer (CEO), Chief Operating Officer (COO) and Chief Financial Officer (CFO). Positions such as Chief Information Officer (CIO), Chief Technology Officer (CTO), Chief Marketing Officer (CMO) and Chief Privacy Officer (CPO) extend this CXX mania and are already largely entrenched in mature companies. With the growth of the service industry in the United States, where employee knowledge is a key asset, a differentiator and value creator for the company, positions such as Chief Knowledge Officer (CKO) and Chief Learning Officer (CLO) are being established. Most recently with the rising recognition that ongoing innovation is the best source of lasting competitive advantage, Chief Innovation Officers (CIO) are being named in Internet companies, like Google, and non-Internet companies alike.

Given high quality, timely data is so vital to driving the success of your company's business processes, why not a Chief Data Officer (CDO)? In this section we will make the case for the Chief Data Officer position and answer the following questions along the way:

- Why a Chief Data Officer for your firm?
- What are her responsibilities?
- What characteristics and skills should you look for in a Chief Data Officer?
- Who should she report to in the organization?
- How do you measure her success?
- What governance and management systems should a Chief Data officer employ?
- Is the Chief Data Officer a permanent position?

Why a Chief Data Officer for Your Firm?

Before you picked up this book, you probably looked at your company data and the role of maintaining it as an enabling function in your information technology department. Yet, the CIO or the Information Technology executive in your company probably spends less than 5% of his time on data and its quality. It's what makes it possible for you to manage your business, but it never makes the new investment priority list above today's urgent needs for revenue growth, quarterly achievement and other traditional systems issues. Like plumbing and electricity, you don't even know it's there until it doesn't work. But putting data quality and data management at the top of your priority list could help you solve some of the other issues that today outrank data. With increasing data quality issues associated with applications that don't effectively exchange data, legal and governmental regulations and the need to pull together data from around your company, it may be time to fix the plumbing.

If you have read up to this point, then hopefully you are convinced of the importance and benefits of having a companywide data strategy and an enterprise data management program. A companywide data management program will improve the data quality used to run your company's current business processes as well as benefit the re-engineering efforts underway in customer relationship management (CRM), supply chain management (SCM), business performance management (BPM) , compliance, privacy and security.

In previous chapters we have made the case that effective enterprise data management is a collaborative effort between IT, business and operations. So, why have a Chief Data Officer?

Companies have known for quite some time that to get something important and broad reaching accomplished, you have to put someone "in charge." So while the success of a companywide data management program requires collaboration and alignment across the company with the business data steward, business unit leaders, information technology and the Corporate Data organization each playing their role, there still needs to be someone "in charge" of driving the overall program—that person is the Chief Data Officer.

The Chief Data Officer is a member of the executive management team of the firm. The CDO serves as the "voice" of data at the executive table where other important business assets are discussed. In 2004, Yahoo was the first company to publicly name a Chief Data Officer, Dr Usama Fayyad. Dr. Fayyad possesses the unique combination of data management and business skills required to be a Chief Data officer. Dr. Fayyad is a recognized leader in the field of data mining and knowledge discovery in databases and has published over 100 technical articles in the fields of artificial intelligence, machine learning, data mining, and databases. Prior to joining Yahoo, Fayyad co-founded two high tech startups in data mining and data strategy consultancy and spent five years at Microsoft building data mining solutions. In one of his first interviews, Dr. Fayyad was quoted as saying "I think Yahoo won't be the first one we see out there, the value of someone to coordinate data use should be

Exhibit 10.1. Roles and Responsibilities of the CDO

Roles	Responsibilities
Data strategist	Define strategic priorities for data systems
	Identify data quality priorities, investments
	Identify new business opportunities pertaining to data
	Optimize revenue generation through data
Data Technology leader	Define the "to-be" technical data architecture, data tools and enterprise data model along with enterprise metadata strategy
Manager of business intelligence and analytic solutions	Define business intelligence infrastructure, technology and tools
Data Steward for companywide business rules, policies and standards	Identify trusted data sources and provide a process for certification of these sources
	Identify mandatory data fields within applications
	Define data management standards and policies
	Provide data retention policies
	Oversee transformation data project requirements for projects that extend across various functions (CRM to ERP, for example)
	Define and classify critical data elements
	Manage enterprise metadata standards and compliance
	Manage security and privacy compliance
Governor of data management	Build governance forums for investment prioritization and issue resolution across business units.
	Manage data policy business tradeoffs
	Manage cross business unit problem resolution of data ownership, funding, data problems
	Manage strategic third-party relationships with data suppliers and outsource firms
Catalyst for driving data ownership and accountability into business units	Identify business data stewards
	Monitor execution of the steward roles
	Establish and enforce business unit accountability for data quality and data management
Data quality leader	Identify enterprise data quality pain points and provide cost/benefit analysis
	Establish data quality targets that align with strategic business goals
	Manage data quality programs with data stewards
	Monitor data quality programs
	Establish data quality assessment program to maintain a consistent, repeatable methodology for analyzing, reporting and prioritizing data quality

Exhibit 10.1. Roles and Responsibilities of the CDO (continued)

Roles	Responsibilities
Architect of the information landscape	Establish an enterprise data architecture and roadmap
	Prioritize implementation of specific enterprise databases
	Monitor simplification program
Partner to Chief Privacy Officer	Monitor data compliance with legal and regulatory requirements such as data privacy and Sarbanes-Oxley
Data asset manager	Define and manage a data asset program that looks at cost, availability, usage and return of all data investments
Member of senior management decision-making, funding body	Ensures that new data investments are consistent with the data strategy and follows defined architectures, standards and tools
	Monitors data projects to ensure objectives are met
System manager	Defines common data management tools, life cycle data management process and drives implementation throughout the enterprise
Change agent	Drive cultural change regarding the importance of data quality as a strategic asset
Profession leader	Establishes an information management profession, including job titles, pay grades consistent with the market, education programs, certification programs, career paths for information management professionals

quite obvious. " He was right. Financial services companies such as Capital One and Citigroup have also named Chief Data Officers. Some companies, uncomfortable using the "Chief Data Officer" title, will use titles such as Senior Vice President or Vice President of Enterprise Data, Data Center of Excellence or Enterprise Data Services. But as Shakespeare so adeptly put it: "A rose by any other name . . . "

What are the Chief Data Officer's Responsibilities?

The Chief Data Officer is responsible for all aspects of data strategy, technology, governance and data management in the firm. As such the roles and responsibilities are broad. The decision on how many of these roles the CDO assumes depends on the company, the urgency of the data management issues and the culture. If your company is in a data crisis, the CDO should assume all the necessary functions to solve it. The basic roles and responsibilities typically assigned to a Chief Data Officer are outlined in Exhibit 10.1.

What are the Skills and Characteristics of the CDO?

One of the challenges companies face in appointing a Chief Data Officer is finding an executive with the right skills. A recent article published in TDAN.com, entitled *Chief Data Steward or Chief Data Officer: Another C-Level Acronym?* , describes the challenges perfectly:

... A Chief Data Officer requires a uniqueness of skill set and personality. The role is not for someone steeped in technical knowledge nor is it for a businessperson who's a technophobe, either. The individual must possess a unique combination of business, technology and diplomatic skills. The role of the CDO must be empowered by the organization to make decisions regarding data, resolving conflicts across disparate groups and establishing enterprise standards on the use of data. The CDO's challenge would be to thoroughly understand the politics within their organizations and have the insight on how to navigate around those challenges.

The Chief Data Officer should have skills grounded in solid data management experience. The CDO should understand data quality management and have experience managing enterprisewide data programs. The CDO must be a visionary who is respected by the executive management in the company. The role requires someone with strong communication skills who can translate complex data topics into business-level discussions and rally the organization to action. The CDO should have general management skills with 15 or more years of experience.

Effective communication skills are also critical to the success of the Chief Data Officer, especially in the first year. With her first year, the CDO should be constantly educating and communicating the business value of data, the need for a comprehensive approach to data management and the need for change in business processes and IT systems. As in all re-engineering initiatives, creating early wins is critical to establishing credibility with her peers and establishing momentum. Equally important is establishing easy-to-understand metrics that can tell the data management progress via the enterprise data management scorecard.

Undoubtedly the role will be new and different for your firm. Because the position will have corporatewide responsibility, the highest levels within your organization must see this as a needed role and be committed to the success of the position. It is recommended that the senior leadership team review the specific roles and responsibilities of the new CDO position and agree to the position before the search

Exhibit 10.2. CDO Reporting Options

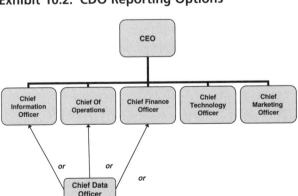

for the candidate begins. At the highest level of the company, any disagreements with the responsibilities and authority placed on the CDO should be resolved before the position is approved. Key members of the executive team who will work as peers to the CDO should interview the CDO candidates. Take your time. Make sure that the candidate is not only qualified for the role, but fits into your culture and with your executive leadership team.

Who Should the Chief Data Officer Report to Within the Organization?

There are several reporting options for the CDO position. The CDO could report to the chief executive officer, the chief financial officer, the chief operating officer or the chief information officer within your company. Who the CDO reports to depends on your company's structure and culture. Roles supporting and reporting to the CDO can include the VP of Content management, Chief Privacy Officer and business data stewards for each major business within the enterprise. There should also be a tight linkage to the General Auditor and to other control functions within the business to ensure the enterprise data strategy supports the regulatory and legal compliance requirements of the firm.

Obviously, the higher in the organization the position reports, the stronger the message of its importance to the firm.

However, we offer a word of caution. Organizations that have their CDO report to the CIO can expect execution challenges. Under the CIO, there is a natural tendency for the firm to view the CDO job as primarily a technical position. Subsequently, data issues are seen as information technology issues when, in fact, the opposite is true. Alternatively, having the position report to the COO or CFO of the firm drives home the message of the importance of business leadership. In some reporting models, the Chief Data Officer will have a dotted-line relationship to the data stewards that exist across the business units and the CIO's data technology organization. In a dotted-line relationship, they would provide functional guidance to those teams and influence the performance rating of the individuals.

Within the corporate data organization that the CDO leads, various organizational structures are possible. The Chief Data officer can lead all aspects of the enterprise data life cycle (Option 1), from strategy inception and governance to development of the enterprise business intelligence and database solutions as well as daily data operations. In Option 2, the CDO may consist of a small team of strategists, architects and project managers who directly lead the enterprise data strategy and the data governance initiatives while data software engineering and database operations reside in the IT organization. Clearly this split necessitates a tight relationship with the CIO and IT teams. Regardless of the organizational structure, the CDO should have ultimate responsibility for all pieces of the data management program, including the operational governance that regularly monitors cost, usage, data policies, practices, quality results and duplication of databases.

Exhibit 10.3. Dotted Line Relationship of CDO to Stewards and Technology

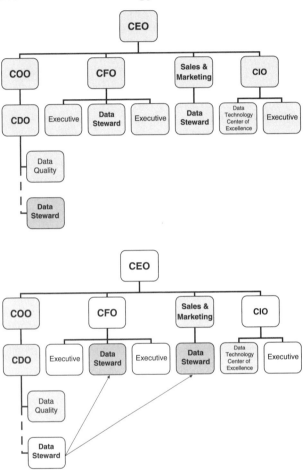

Exhibit 10.4. Option 1: Full Data Lifecycle Management

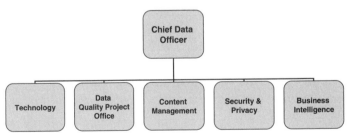

Exhibit 10.5. Option 2: Data Strategy—Governance

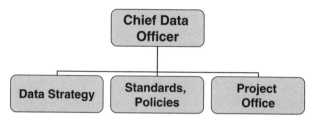

What are Some Measurements of Success for the CDO?

As the Chief Data Officer position is new, few best practices for measuring success are available. Exhibit 10.6 shows some measurements to consider.

Exhibit 10.6. Metrics for Measuring Success

Measures of Success	Metrics
Data responsibilities, requirements and accountabilities clearly understood	• Data steward assigned in key areas • Functional senior managers know and value data steward role • Data targets integrated into employee goals
Data investments made in support of company-wide data strategy	• Data investments approved by CDO • No rogue data programs
Data supports all legal, privacy and business requirements	• No SOX violations • Positive internal audit reviews • No privacy data issues or leaks
Business data policies and standards in place and followed	• Compliance to standards is measured annually • High compliance to standards
Data issues are identified and resolved in design phases of new projects	• Data problems are tracked in 1 place • Data problems found at design phase. Resolution does not impact schedule or budget
Cost and benefits of data understood	• TCO metrics in place • TCO reduced each year
Data quality program in place and yielding results	• Data quality metrics in place • Data quality improving each year
Data is viewed as an asset	• CDO position valued by CXO • All of the above metrics in place and active

Is the Chief Data Officer a Permanent Position?

Yes—at least for the foreseeable future!!

Appointing Business Data Stewards

Exhibit 10.7. Data Stewardship Defined

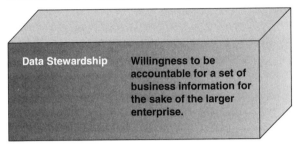

| Data Stewardship | Willingness to be accountable for a set of business information for the sake of the larger enterprise. |

Another important new leadership position in the overall enterprise data management program is the Business Data Steward. As the name implies, the business data steward is the business leader responsible for "stewarding" the critical data within their business or function, be it the data the business creates, buys or uses. From an overall enterprise data governance perspective, the business data steward formalizes the accountability in the business for the definition, accuracy, consistency and timeliness of the critical information within a specified data scope.

In Larry's English book , *Improving Data Warehouse and Business Information Quality*, information stewardship is defined as "the willingness to be accountable for a set of business information for the well-being of the larger organization by operating in service, rather than in control, of those around us." The key words here are "operating in service" as stewards are not "owners" of the business data. The true owners of the data are the stakeholders of the company.

In this section, we make the case for the business data steward and answer these questions:

- Why should you have a business data steward within each business?
- How should you think about the role and its mission?
- What are the attributes of a good business data steward?
- How can you ensure the business data steward is successful?

Why Do You Need a Business Data Steward?

Hopefully by now, we have convinced you of the rationale for managing data as a business asset consistent with the other business assets in the firm. As we have said repeatedly in previous chapters, data drives business processes and data helps business people make business decisions. Business data makes it possible for business processes to "talk" to each other in a digital way. Customer data lets customers "talk" to you. When applied in an analytical and business intelligence scenario, data can drive new business value. Therefore, as data is a business enabler, it should be assigned a business owner that will apply business judgment to the decisions made from and with the data. That someone is the business data steward. The business data steward is the voice of her business unit to the enterprise. When selecting a business data steward, it is advisable to appoint a leader from within the business unit or functional area where the business process is executed and where the majority of the data for which the business data steward will manage is created. Here are some examples:

- Supply chain business data steward: Sr. VP, Demand Management & Planning
- Finance data steward : CFO or Finance/Accounting executive
- Marketing data steward: Chief Marketing Officer or Marketing Intelligence executive
- Product data steward: Lab product manager
- Employee data steward : Head of Human Resources
- Customer data steward: Head of Corporate Sales

Not all data requires a business data steward, but certainly all critical data should be assigned a business data steward. The responsibility for the overall business data stewardship program lies with the Chief Data Officer, Head of Corporate Data or the Chief Operating Officer. They should first determine the critical data areas in the company for which a steward is needed. There are times when an enlightened operations executive acts on his own to name a business data steward for his particular business unit to address the data issues specific to their organization. This action is rare because the steward role is not generally well understood nor is it accepted by the business. In some cases, where the data and processes for a particular type of data are dispersed, such as customer data, the position could reside in multiple organizations. Sales, marketing or operations could steward customer data. The goal is to assign the stewardship as high and as visible as possible, because this position will need to be respected across the firm in order to drive the data programs across multiple organizations. While the leaders of the Corporate Data organization identify the domains for which the stewards are needed, they should not name the stewards themselves. The heads of each of the businesses where the stewards will report should name specific individuals.

Because stewardship is a new and evolving role in organizations, it is generally believed that less than half of large companies have a formal data stewardship program. Many large corporations, however, are implementing some level of data governance driven by the recent Sarbanes-Oxley Act of 2002. While standard practices in stewardship are emerging, your company should tailor the role to meet the culture, information maturity and data issues in your firm. In some companies, the business data steward is an executive position; in other organizations, it is not. In some organizations, a corporate data team is in place; in some places, it is not. In some companies, business process owners exist and provide much-needed business process expertise to the business data stewards; in some companies, these roles are nonexistent. In some businesses, data stewards are responsible for specific *"data*

Exhibit 10.8.Data Fields for "Customer"

Customer	Prospect	Suspect
Business Name	Business Name	
Address	Address	
Email Address	Email Address	Email Address
Standard industry code	Standard industry code	
Purchases		
Responses to marketing, sales inquiries	Responses to marketing	Responses to marketing

objects," such as customer, partner, bookings, etc. These objects and their use throughout the business is the responsibility of the steward assigned.

A data object is simply all the information associated with defining an entity. For example, to define "customer" in a business-to-business situation, you may need the following data fields associated with the object of "customer":

- Business name
- Address
- Standard industry code
- Purchases

Other fields could also be applied depending on whether you differentiate between customer, suspect and prospect within your databases. Exhibit 10.8 shows a comparison of the data fields that could be used for each variation of "customer."

In the "data object" implementation, the business data steward reaches across functional lines to manage the data in the "object." For example, in managing the customer purchases data element, the Customer Object business data steward may reach out to Accounts Receivable. For managing responses to marketing and sales inquiries, they may confer with the Marketing and Sales organizations.

How Should You Think About Business Data Stewards and Their Mission?

A Business Data Steward is a leadership position that understands the importance of data to their part of the business. Usually the business data steward is someone for whom data quality has a direct impact on his or her job. For example, the SOX (Sarbanes-Oxley) compliance officer may be the business data steward for financial data because he understands the implications of good data to maintaining SOX compliance. Just as you have business managers who manage people and product managers who manage your product portfolio, the business data steward manages

Exhibit 10.9. Activities of the Business Data Steward

Task	Example
Translate business unit strategy into data tactics that achieve the business objective.	If the manufacturing business unit strategy is to build zero-defect products, then: • Data collected and managed by this unit should make it possible to effectively monitor and track product defects. • Supply chain data steward would work with the procurement organization to establish and enforce product quality targets from suppliers. • Supply chain data steward drives programs to enable product manufacturing processes to capture and report product defect in real time before the product leaves the factory.
Identify the critical, high-value data that the business needs. Decide what data is needed, when and how it should be available to effectively manage the business.	If the service department of a cable television company requires real-time information regarding product installation in order to deliver against the business objective of 100% customer satisfaction, then the customer data steward is responsible for ensuring that the data is available to customer service representatives and their managers as soon as the cable goes online at a customer site. The business data steward should also ensure that the data is accessible to those individuals responsible for customer satisfaction.
When new data is created or sourced for the business, gain consensus on the common definition of the data element and its allowable values. Drive the usage of that common business terminology across all required processes and systems.	If the chief marketing officer decides that new customer acquisition is a mandatory requirement for reaching the business objectives for the year, then the marketing data steward is responsible for helping the organization define "new" customer. Will it be an individual who has never purchased from your company before, even though the individual belongs to a company that has done business with you in the past? Or will it be a company previously unknown to your database that purchases a product? The steward is responsible not only for driving a common definition, but ensuring that all systems and processes use the same definition. • Marketing's business data steward works with the business data stewards in sales and customer service to ensure these systems make the required changes.
For new data created or sourced within a business unit, ensure that the data meets the needs of all users and that it adheres to regulatory as well as internal audit requirements.	• If the finance department's objectives for the year include being able to report to the market on the number of customers acquired by vertical market, then the finance business data steward works with the marketing business data steward to ensure that the company has an agreed-to definition of vertical market internally as well as one that can be agreed to externally. The steward needs also to ensure that all processes for acquiring and managing this data can be audited should the need arise. • If one marketing organization needs to purchase D&B customer data for a particular marketing analysis, an effective marketing data steward will know, via the enterprise metadata, whether that data has already been purchased by another department in marketing or elsewhere across the firm. This knowledge helps to direct the marketing department to where the D&B data already exists and saves the company the expense of repurchasing.

Exhibit 10.9. Activities of the Business Data Steward (continued)

Task	Example
Quantify and prioritize data quality issues based on business pain points. For data created or sourced within the business unit, drive overall data quality improvement plans working across the business, with IT and enterprise data initiatives.	• One of the truths of data quality mentioned earlier is: "Data quality, like beauty, is in the eye of the beholder." By that we mean each business process has unique data quality requirements for the data it uses. The business data steward's knowledge of the business processes within their function helps determine those specific data quality requirements. They accomplish this by working in concert with the business process owners. In addition to identifying the specific accuracy, completeness, validity and timeliness requirements of the data within a process, the business data steward determines the priority of these different dimensions of data quality to further refine the prioritization of the data initiatives. For example, the product data steward might most likely prioritize improving the timeliness of the product price data reaching the product Web catalog over any other data quality dimensions. The marketing data steward, however, might prioritize improving the completeness and accuracy of email customer information for marketing campaign process effectiveness.
Drive business process changes to improve data effectiveness and quality within the business.	• If one of the objectives for sales is to make sales calls on executives higher within an organization, then the data steward for sales may be asked to help the sales organization acquire and manage data that identifies the top executive within a company. As a result of the data steward's work, the sales representative has information on who within the company has been contacted previously by your sales department. • If sales reps are not required to enter contact information, the data steward needs to work with sales management to ensure that the customer relationship management processes includes gathering this information, evaluating its quality and establishing processes for ensuring that quality is maintained.
Catalog and organize data so that it is easily accessible by business users. Determine what data archive strategy best fits the business.	• Finance may require that only certain accumulated information be stored. • Service may require transactional-level information storage. • Marketing and Corporate Strategy often require keeping information as far back as 10 to 20 years for analytic, planning and audit purposes. • The archive strategy may also be influenced by regulatory requirements such as external financial reporting and customer privacy and security. Regulatory requirements may dictate not just for how long the data must be stored, but in what medium and in what location.

Exhibit 10.9. Activities of the Business Data Steward (continued)

Task	Example
Drive the consolidation and simplification of the database landscape within the business.	• Many data pain points are the result of too many databases containing redundant information populated throughout the organization. While business managers often think that the best way to manage their data is to develop their own databases, these rogue data sources often represent the greatest challenge to an enterprise-level data strategy. Because they are managed as islands of information, building bridges from one database to another can be difficult and often impossible. Without a bridge, one part of the business may not be able to talk to another part. • For example, if manufacturing develops a system that assigns customers a number that is unrelated to the one assigned by sales, executives may be challenged in understanding what products were shipped to which customers or partners. • When business managers want to build or acquire a new database, they should first seek the data steward's advice. The task of consolidating redundant, underused databases falls on the business data steward working in concert with their information technology teams.

the portfolio of business data. To accomplish this task, the business data steward must lead and orchestrate the following activities outlined in Exhibit 10.9.

Business data stewards affect change in business processes, technology systems and governance in order to ensure the business data objectives can be met. Often this requires that they work together across business units. For example, if the business sells a business unit, each business unit needs to evaluate its processes to ensure that the data exchanged between these units is effectively and accurately disentangled. Financial reporting will change. Product and customer reporting may change. Business data stewards are responsible for orchestrating and directing this activity to a workable and working conclusion.

The business data steward also needs the support of senior business managers to carry out the re-engineering of business processes. Manual data entry processes in the business are usually the areas of highest data quality errors. Defining and implementing an automated business process falls on the business data steward working in concert with the business process owner.

The business data steward similarly influences or directly develops the appropriate business processes, including incentives and penalties in the contracts, to ensure external providers of data—whether they be a customer, a business partner or an external data vendor—provide consistent, high-quality data per the agreed upon service-level agreement .

What are the Attributes of an Effective Business Data Steward?

An effective business data steward is an effective leader, communicator and team builder *first* and *foremost*:

- She understands the priorities and strategies of the business unit she represents and can translate those into data priorities and strategies for the business.
- She commands respect within the organization. A business data steward must be a change agent. To accomplish this, she needs to be well-respected and integrated into the business unit.
- She builds consensus across a varied set of business priorities and agendas. A data steward is both business manager and politician. Driving consensus across the organization is as essential as it is important.
- She influences and drives changes to business processes to improve overall effectiveness and efficiencies. She must look at data as integral to driving these changes.
- She enjoys strong support from the senior business leaders within her business unit. To enforce decisions, the most senior leaders within the business must trust and support the business data steward.
- She can effectively communicate to business and technical teams alike the need for change and the importance of the data initiatives.
- She can build a diverse team of technical and business data experts to resolve data issues.

Exhibit 10.10. Attributes of an Effective Business Data Steward

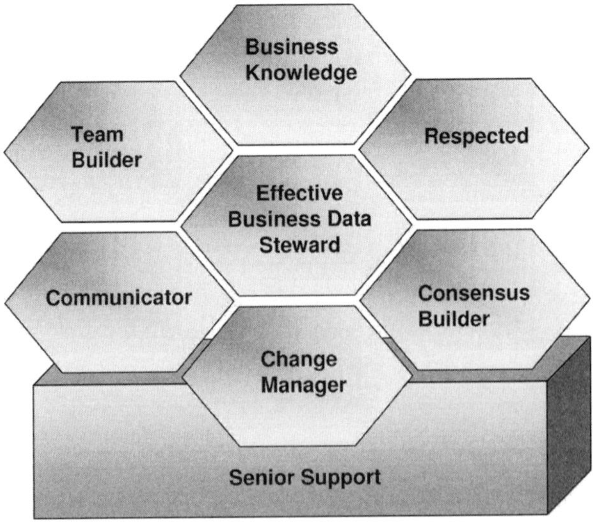

What Level is the Business Data Steward and to Whom Does the Steward Report?

It is highly recommended that the business data steward be an executive in your company. Having an executive in this position sends a powerful message to the organization as to the seriousness of the company's commitment to its data and, subsequently, the importance of this role.

When assigning an executive to the role, some companies use the term "Executive Business Data Steward" and reserve the term "business data steward" to denote stewards for particular data domains within the team. For example, if a company named a Supply Chain Executive Data Steward, then within the supply chain there may also be a procurement business data steward and a manufacturing business data steward. Each of these stewards may not hold an executive position. The Executive Data Steward is responsible for the overall deployment of the information management, data quality programs and stewardship programs in her organization. She provides executive "air cover" to the business data stewards and ensures they have the resources, decision-making accountability and access to the business leaders. This makes doing their jobs easier and possible.

Be advised, while an executive business data steward is not necessarily a full-time assignment, especially if the executive is a vice president or above, a business data steward *is* a full-time position. There is much to do, especially in the start-up phase. Assigning the task to individuals who already have a full-time job is a formula for failure. A business data steward drives the implementation of the data quality and information management programs for their data. Hence, a person with senior business data analyst experience is often ideally suited for this position. The person should understand data models and "data tech talk," but also bridge the gap between business and technology to the business leaders.

Exhibit 10.11. Data Steward Reporting Options

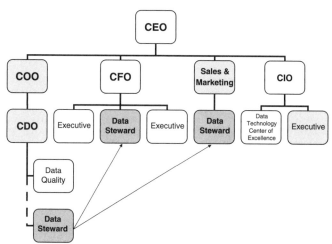

Getting Started with Limited Resources

Often companies resist implementing a business data steward program in the organization because they believe they cannot afford to divert additional resources or dollars to a stewardship program. It takes a strong senior business leader, like you, to break this cycle of thinking. There is always someone on your leadership team who has shown a passion for data. He or she has probably provided a voice for data in the past and may have even recommended this type of role. Conversely, there are always leaders who are ready for a new challenge or a new assignment. Take the leap, appoint a leader today.

Now you have your business data steward!

Once the leader is on board, she needs to build a team of data experts for the data that needs managing. This too, can be done incrementally. Usually data experts exist in the organization, but often reside in different teams across the function. They either are currently performing a business data analyst role or working on data quality for a specific project. The business data steward has two organizational alternatives: (1) establish a "virtual" team of these data experts, or (2) collect these data experts in one organization under the leadership of the business data steward. Here again, the business data steward must rely on the support of the senior business leader because critical data experts are not easily given up by their existing management. Only after the business data steward has accumulated the current individuals doing "steward-like" roles into the business data steward team should they begin to evaluate adding additional resources to the team.

How to Ensure a Successful Business Data Stewardship Program in Your Organization

- Name business data stewards in phases. Name the most critical data stewards first.
- Appoint business data stewards as close to the business process as possible.
- Ensure executive business sponsorship and access.
- Empower the business data steward to directly address issues with noncompliance to a data standard or data policy.
- Provide resources, tools and training to ensure success of the business data steward.
- Establish performance metrics and ongoing communication with business executives.
- Ensure business data stewards have access to business unit strategies and key leadership forums.
- Ensure partnership with the Enterprise Data organization.
- Communicate business data steward successes broadly in the organization.
- Encourage business data stewards to keep their solutions practical and pragmatic and, above all, tied to business objectives and pain points.
- Provide training and ongoing support.

Training the Business Data Steward

As business data stewards become more prevalent in companies, courses from information management consulting companies are increasingly available to train new data stewards. One such education program is entitled Enterprise Data Stewardship & Governance: Full Life-Cycle Roadmap. The course is offered through EW Solutions-Marco Masters Series and provides a certification upon completion of the class. The Web site is: *http://www.ewsolutions.com/news-events/marco-masters-series*. The course description and seminar outline are shown in Exhibit 10.12.

Exhibit 10.12. EW Solutions Data Governance Course

Course Description:

This *EWSolutions*-certified course provides participants with practical, in-depth understanding of how to implement a successful enterprise-wide data governance and stewardship program. Through case studies and team interaction, attendees will attain the real-world implementation skills necessary to build a program for their organization. Attendees will receive examples of the various artifacts that form the documentation of a data governance and stewardship program, and will be able to interact with other attendees to extend their understanding of the importance of starting and maintaining an enterprise-wide data governance and stewardship program. Hands-on workshops throughout the course will reinforce the learning experience and provide the attendees with concrete results that can be used in their organizations.

Seminar Outline:

1. Understanding How to Convert Data into Information
2. How to Properly Manage Data as a Corporate Asset
3. Enterprise Data Management and Governance
   How to Set Attainable Objectives
   Define Scalable Data Management Functions
4. Introduction to Data Governance
   Issues and Challenges of Implementing a Data Governance Program
   Key Attributes to a Successful Data Governance Program
   Role of the Data Governance Program in Enterprise Data Management
5. Introduction to Data Stewardship
   Understand the Four Types of Data Stewards
   Learn to Identify the Right People to Become Data Stewards
   Issues and Challenges of Data Stewardship
   Key Attributes of Successful Data Stewards
   Role of the Data Stewardship in a Data Governance Program
6. Implementing a Data Governance and Stewardship Program
   Defining Governance Requirements

Identifying Data and Meta Data Sources
Approaches to Data Governance Development
Creating the Governance Team
Integrating Data Stewardship into a Data Governance Program
Creating the Governance and Stewardship Project Plan
Constructing Appropriate Governance Documents
Planning the Maintenance of a Data Governance and Stewardship Program
Future of Data Governance and Stewardship
7. Implementing a Data Governance and Stewardship Program
Key Pitfalls to Avoid
How to Break Down Political Barriers
How to Implement Your Program in Manageable Iterations
8. Conclusion, Discussion, References for Additional Study

What Governance and Management Systems Should a Chief Data Officer Employ?

The Chief Data Officer is ultimately responsible for execution of the enterprise data management strategy across the firm. Yet, as we have discussed, successful execution requires all players in the firm to do their parts, including business leaders, technical departments, business data stewards and operations. Often, the challenge for the CDO is that these organizations do not directly report into her. In fact, in most cases these organizations belong to executives who are her peers and who have their own priorities. So how does the CDO drive collaboration and alignment? Data governance is the vehicle.

In a recent CIO article titled *Six Steps to Data Governance Success*,[1] the author describes data governance:

> . . . . *Data governance as a political challenge requires building consensus among many diverse stakeholders. Political leadership within the organization is therefore a priority.*
>
> *Establish a governing council composed of organizational stakeholders to formulate stewardship policies and report progress to the CEO and board of directors.*

No doubt, the political challenges for the Chief Data Officer are huge. Why? First, companies' data issues have taken many years to develop and will take multiple years to fix. To add to this, most organizations' tolerance for multi-year programs is quite low. Second, business leaders and IT leaders alike have an opinion on how the data issues are to be fixed and they usually assume it is the other organizations' responsibility. Third, data quality issues are fundamentally data management

---

[1] *Six Steps to Data Governance Success* by Steve Adler, www.cio.com, May 31 2007.

deficiencies scattered throughout the companies' processes and systems. The immediate reaction of most companies is to jump at "patching up" the data quality problem by fixing it in a database. This leads to *not* working on the root causes of the data management deficiencies that create data quality issues in the first place. Finally, data management is a complex, new subject for managers. Explaining it to business and IT leaders with simple, relevant language is an art form and requires persistence. More than any other function in business, data management is a true balance between art and science.

To tackle these political challenges, one of the first governance steps recommended for a new CDO is establishing a forum of executive peers from across the company. Whether the forum is a voting board or an advisory board does not matter. The goal is to ensure a broad, inclusive membership.

At a minimum, the forum should provide advice to the Chief Data Officer in the following areas:

1. Scoping the data to be managed by the enterprise data management program:
   - Structured data in databases
   - Unstructured data in emails and documents
   - Analytic data
   - Metadata
   - Content data (Web)

2. Establishing enterprise data yearly priorities:
   - Improve data quality
   - Attain "single version of truth"
   - Improve productivity
   - Increase revenue
   - Improve reporting
   - Improve security and privacy compliance
   - Improve data controls
   - Improve reusability and manage redundancy
   - Reduce total cost of operations

3. Reviewing enterprise data policies and standards
   - Security
   - Privacy
   - Metadata
   - Data quality
   - Create/Maintain/Delete (CRUD) critical data

4. Reviewing key enterprise data investments and programs:
   - Enterprise data quality
   - Master and Reference Data
   - Enterprise Metadata

- Business Data Steward programs
- Information management tools
- Enterprise data services
- Information management profession and education

5. Identifying and resolving cross business unit data issues:
   - Data sharing
   - Data quality responsibilities
   - Data definition differences

6. Prioritizing enterprise data quality investments

7. Establishing and reviewing enterprise data scorecard and metrics

The executive forum is an important venue for addressing these political challenges, but clearly is not the only venue the CDO should use. Senior level management—CEO, COO, CIO and CFO—must stand behind the Chief Data Officer, providing air cover during resistance as well as opportunities for public endorsement. Conversely, in order to gain that level of support, the Chief Data Officer must provide ongoing communication on the progress of the program to the senior-level managers and gain their confidence that the programs are practical, pragmatic and focused.

A working forum can also be established for the business data stewards , chaired by the corporate data organization. The business data steward forum is a different forum from the executive forum chaired by the CDO herself. Both forums, however, *are* part of the overall management system the CDO should employ. The executive forum deals with investment decisions, policies and direction-setting. The stewardship council manages more detail-oriented projects, covering topics such as critical data term identification, data term definition, data quality business rules, and enterprise data models. The stewardship council also serves in a staff position to vet data issues and provide recommendations to the executive data forum for issues they cannot solve.

Data governance is an ongoing program. It is not a one-time event launched at the beginning of the Chief Data Officer's tenure. As such, dedicated resources are required to keep the governance program going. The data governance office establishes the meeting agendas, drives the staff work before and after the meeting, tracks work items and the enterprise data management metrics. These are examples of just a few of the tasks assigned to the data governance team. Data governance office (DGO) staff facilitates impact analysis and issue resolution work sessions. Equally important, the data governance office acts as a single point of contact for enterprise data governance within the CDO's organization, where key governance decisions and changes are communicated.

A Matrix Organization:
Business Data Steward and Chief Data Officer

The business data steward cannot be left alone in the business unit. To enable the business data stewards to effectively do their job, a Corporate Data organization reporting to the CDO should provide an overall framework for stewardship. This framework includes tools, enterprise policies, standards, best practices and enterprise-level data governance to resolve issues and set priorities. The Corporate Data organization also chairs the governance forum consisting of all the data stewards identified within the corporation. In the business data steward forum, the council reviews enterprise data policies and standards, resolves issues that cross organizations and manages changes to the enterprise metadata. In this forum, the Corporate Data organization also acts as a "chief steward." The Corporate Data organization determines the number of stewards needed and establishes a clear delineation of the data each steward manages, resolving conflicts over the stewardship of all data elements. The Corporate Data organization also covers any data "white spaces" not covered by a steward. For example, if the corporation acquires companies often, the Corporate Data organization may be exclusively responsible for the integration of the acquired company's data. The Corporate Data organization also establishes a way to measure and track each steward's progress. This often requires the establishment of a set of consistent, balanced metrics that are communicated via a data scorecard. While companies have established business data stewardship without an overall Corporate Data organization, the tasks performed by the corporate data team are invaluable to the success of data stewards. Without a group in the company providing this service to the stewards, the stewards are left on their own to develop these programs. The results are, at best, inconsistent.

There exists a mutually beneficial governance relationship between the business data steward and the Corporate Data organization. While the business data steward needs the corporate data team to provide her with tools, techniques and an overall governance framework to help orchestrate her effectiveness within the business unit, the Corporate Data organization needs the business data steward to drive the enterprise data policies, standards and strategies into the business unit data. The Corporate Data organization and the business data stewards should see themselves as members of the same companywide data team.

Assessing and Measuring Progress of
Data Management Maturity

An emerging technique a CDO can use for demonstrating a companies' progress in enterprise data management is an information management maturity assessment. Maturity assessment models are available from data tool and consulting companies such as IBM and DataFlux (a SAS company). The Data Warehousing Institute (TDWI), an educational institute for data warehousing and business intelligence,

Exhibit 10.13. IBM Maturity Model with Data Governance

Exhibit 10.14. Comparison of Three Data Governance Models

Model	IBM	Dataflux	TDWI
# of Stages	5	4	6
Stages	1. Initial	1. Undisciplined	1. Prenatal
	2. Managed	2. Reactive	2. Infant
	3. Defined	3. Proactive	3. Child
	4. Quantitatively	4. Governed	4. Teenager
	5. Optimizing		5. Adult
			6. Sage
Contact information	*www.ibm.com*	*www.dataflux.com*	*www.tdwi.com*

also provides a maturity model and benchmarking guide. The models are similar and employ a multi-stage maturity scale with between four to six stages. The assessment is based on answers to a set of survey questions. Parameters measured in the survey include data architecture, data stewardship, data governance, business value perceived, organizational awareness, executive commitment and data controls. The multi-point scale is similar to the five-point software engineering SEI rating used to rate the maturity of software organizations in software development techniques.

The IBM model above provides one example of a maturity model (see Exhibit 10.13).

The assessment can be completed as a self-assessment or consultation services are available. Once completed, the companies can also provide consulting services to address how to improve the company's data management program.

These assessments tools are relatively new and still evolving. We suspect more consulting companies will offer their own customized versions. The benefits of this technique, while still new, does provide a consistent, repeatable process for assessing data management progress based on a cross-industry set of enterprise data management parameters.

Data Management Scorecard

Another way of measuring and reporting progress on the enterprise data management program is through an enterprise data management balanced scorecard or by including key metrics in the companywide balanced scorecard. While imperfect at measuring all aspects of data management maturity, the scorecard can capture key indicators of progress that can be trended and reported to business leaders and senior executive management alike. Examples of indicators to include in the scorecard:

- Number of databases
- Number of open data issues
- Databases documented in the enterprise metadata repository
- Database storage utilization
- Data quality improvement
- Data standards compliance
- Open audit reports due to identified data deficiencies
- Open data control exposures
- Total cost of data operations
- Total cost of data quality
- Data system availability and usage
- Number of certified information management professionals

Summary

The role of data and the governance of it by business data stewards and chief data officers is evolving. Just as change is the constant we can count on, requirements for managing data as a corporate asset will change as well. In the next five to ten years, the next challenge for CDOs will be making it possible for the owner or user of an information source to maintain and manage the data without the information management organization. We will coin and make real a new term—Self-service data.

This will require that your company's customers and employees be given the ability to manage data on their own. At least, they should be allowed to manage that data asset that reflects information about them. This should enable you to provide better customer service. Here are some ways in which data management will change in the next ten years:

1. Customer information retained by the company, managed by the customer.
2. Data derived from applications that is kept for only the time required to

enable the transaction (such as Web information). Instant use, instant dele-
tion may be forced by society's growing requirement for privacy.

3. Data assets that know when they should be archived and manage their own
   archive routine.
4. Utilizing artificial intelligence—systems that automatically edit data upon
   entry—for not only validity, but accuracy as well.
5. Architectures that allow for data insight to be gleaned easily and readily
   from data warehouses, making data available to all aspects of the business.
6. Systems that evaluate the accuracy of business intelligence models immediately upon their use in the application and report automatically on lift or
   shift.
7. Utilizing an employee rating system—for example, social tagging—to judge
   the usefulness of a company's data and ultimately to improve the user-per-
   ceived quality of the data.

These examples of the future data management environment highlight the
need for a different approach to managing this type of asset and, ultimately, lead to
the conclusion that some organizations are already reaching: Once you have a Chief
Data Officer, there is much to do now and in the future.

For More Information

The Data Governance Institute is an independent organization that provides training,
consulting and publications on data governance and data stewards. The institute's
Web site provides a wealth of free information on tools, techniques, best practices and
standards. For more information, go to: *http://www.datagovernance.com/index.html.*

11

Get Talent:
Securing the Right Data Skills

The Business Data Steward and the Chief Data Officer do not work alone. They need talented information professionals on their team. What's most common in business is to take a good business operations or financial analyst, give them a few hours of training, change their job title and tell them to "fix the data problem." You wouldn't take a marketing person without an accounting background and make them a financial analyst. They won't have the training. The same is true of the information management skill. It takes three to five years of managing information programs before a competency is developed.

However, don't think that technical skill is sufficient. Most technical skills in organizations today lack "business" acumen. Often individuals titled database analysts understand the physical requirements of a database design, but may not understand business drivers or when and how to involve business leaders in developing data policies and procedures. They perpetuate keeping the technical team as the sole driver of these policies and procedures. That's a mistake.

On the business side, many information projects are led by Marketing or Finance leaders who fail to grasp the pitfalls of a bad technical design. As a result, they often develop many databases with no supporting data quality programs. They drive for accelerated schedules that skip all the necessary data design, analysis and life cycle management. Their projects may deploy on time and may even provide valuable information once deployed, but often are not sustainable because the proper life cycle programs were not implemented or, in most cases, even conceived.

You need both skills—technical and business—to successfully manage a database or data quality project. If you have individuals in your organization who have the technical, business and change management skills combined, treasure them. They are or will be in hot demand. A recent search on Monster.com for "information management" yielded over 700 opportunities. The marketplace for information management professionals is, indeed, hot.

Don't have any individuals in your organization who can use information to address business requirements? Have a lot of data and technical people who may or may not have all the requirements? Then, consider hiring information management professionals, as retraining will take you several years. The information management professional is the conduit and relationship manager between the business and IT. They also make good business data stewards.

Skills of the Information Management Professional

An effective information management professional has the following skills:

- Knowledgeable of current business processes and how business processes relate to one another. Also understands the data used by those processes. If you must hire this skill from the outside, make sure that you give the IM professional time to absorb the nuances of your business before you give the go-ahead to implement major changes.

- Understands and communicates how information systems support business strategies. Communication is the key here. An IM professional who cannot communicate is a liability. Primarily, they must be able to take very complex issues, simplify them and express them in ways that ordinary, non-data people can understand.

- Knowledgeable of data management, data architecture and data quality best practices.

- Ensures alignment of data systems to business transformation initiatives. Can produce "use cases" or scenarios of how the business will use the data.

- Uses industry best practices to create business data models.

- Understands the differences between various types of data stores (operational data store, master data, data warehouse, data mart) and how those differences affect the business requirements.

- Can efficiently capture and represent both the business side and software development side of a data application or systems solution.

- Bridges the gap between business architect and application architect.

- Knowledgeable of all databases in the firm. Identifies ways to efficiently share and reuse information across the enterprise.

- Can design ways to ensure information is easily and readily accessed and used.

- Can develop information work flows.

The information management role is as essential as the business data steward. They are important partners. The business data steward is responsible for managing the content in the data stores, data warehouses and data marts, specifically its:

- Accuracy and quality
- Adherence to standards
- Ease of access
- Appropriate levels of summarization, derivation and aggregation for reporting and management purposes

Supported by the information management professional, the business data steward's job is doable. Without the IM professional, the job disintegrates to a clerical data input and cleanup exercise. Today, in most enterprises, the roles of data stewards and information management professionals are often underestimated and, as a consequence, underinvested in and mismanaged. When an executive begins to manage across several lines of business, the need for a business data steward and information management professional surfaces for one outstanding reason—the requirement to provide metrics and measurements across business units or siloed operations. The value that an IM professional brings to these projects is that he or she understands the broad uses of data within the company and manages data as an corporate asset—taking a unique view of the business and the technology that supports it. Information management professionals not only support the technology for aspects such as reporting, but they also provide standards for data governance, tool evaluation, new technologies and partnerships with process professionals. An information management professional is crucial when merging two companies' data after an acquisition.

An effective information management professional has expertise in many areas, including:

- Application design
- Business reporting and analytics design
- Written and presentation communication skills
- Business area analysis
- Data modeling and the ability to read both logical and physical data models
- Database design
- Business data analysis
- Business design
- Information work flow and process design
- Business use case (scenario) development
- Project management
- Understanding of the company's business goals and processes such as financial management, sales opportunity management, etc.
- Consulting skills
- Tools evaluation capability
- Metadata management
- Analytic skills

To Certify or Not to Certify?

When building a data management organization, you may face the challenge of verifying that your team has the requisite skills. Here's one way to attack this issue:

1. Determine the skills that you need for a high performance information management team.
2. Inventory the skills that you have on-board.
3. Determine the gaps between your existing team and your visionary one.
4. Implement a specific training program that addresses those gaps or hire new talent with the required skills.

One of the ways to ensure that you keep the skills of your key team members growing is to implement a certification program. These programs can be specifically designed for your organization or you can enlist a professional organization or university to support you in your efforts. Certification or specialization gives you the ability to identify those individuals who are most interested and passionate about information management and to pinpoint those who are truly the leaders in the area. When you consult your human resources department about certification or specialization, be prepared to address the issues associated with reward and career development.

True certification programs that are managed internally may not be completely supported by your HR departments because of the expense of audits and any legal ramifications associated with internal certification. A better alternative may be to work jointly with a local university or college to identify courses that would fit your specific requirements. As part of your employee training program, you can require that employees take classes and work toward a certification program offered by the educational institution. This allows your company to take advantage of the training and skills that result without the hassle and expense of establishing an internal certification program.

The Data Warehousing Institute (TDWI) has recently begun certifying business analysts. Their new certification includes education and testing in information systems, business metrics and visualization of information in addition to basic statistics. David Wells, Director of Education for TDWI, says that his organization had received so many inquiries from firms that needed to standardize skills of business analysts that they implemented this program in response to market demand. Although the market has yet to embrace certification as a way to differentiate potential employees in the hiring process, you can well imagine that this may one day be a prerequisite advertised for when seeking key employees.

But, let's suppose you find that securing the skills required for your information management department is extremely difficult or that you are in an industry where these skills are highly sought after and expensive. Either one of these situations may require that you establish an internal certification program and market it as a competitive advantage for your company. Often these types of programs attract college hires from the better schools because they see the possibilities of continued improvement and the company's investment in them.

Summary

Whether you are building a data management discipline or have inherited one, you may need to evaluate the individual skills of information management professionals. Getting clear on what you want to accomplish and how may help you establish a solid mission for these individuals. Data management is a competency; treat it as such with the appropriate HR programs, certification and career paths. Information management professionals are becoming hot commodities in the marketplace because of the growing need to manage data at an enterprise level. Making them feel the skill is valued will keep them in your company.

12

Communicate and Educate: Selling Data and Overcoming Resistance

Not everyone in the organization will be thrilled with the installation of a Chief Data Officer or the implementation of a data management plan for the entire company. There will be those who are negative about the plan and, still more troubling, there will be passive-aggressive resistance to some of the work that must be done. This chapter helps you to understand where the resistance might originate, what drives it and how you can help overcome it.

Changing Attitudes About Data

Changing employees' behaviors and attitudes around data is one of the hardest leadership challenges faced by anyone in charge of data initiatives. So what behaviors and attitudes must change, you ask? Exhibit 12.1 provides a quick look at the task you have at hand.

Ensuring that these attitudes and behaviors change necessitates different techniques. While the executive and stewardship forums created by the Chief Data Officer may certainly help by ensuring key executives model the appropriate behaviors toward data, the attitudes and behavior of *all* employees have to be modified. Everyone that buys, creates, changes and handles data needs to understand these new ways of thinking. More importantly, they need to act out the new behavior in their everyday interactions with the data.

Changing attitudes and behaviors involves selling, communicating to and educating groups who you must convert to the data management movement. Assessing your constituents' potential acceptance of the data management strategy is helpful in mapping out a tailored approach. The first group that must be converted was discussed in Chapter 7.

The senior executives must be won over early because you depend on their support. Without their support, it is very difficult to gain traction on any broad data initiative.

Exhibit 12.1. Necessary Changes in Attitudes About Data

Old Attitude	New Attitude
Data issues are IT issues.	Data issues are business process and data management issues scattered across business process and systems that IT just happens to manage.
Data is "owned" by the organization that generates it or acquires its.	Data is not "owned" by any single group, but rather is a strategic company asset that must be cared for by the company's business data stewards.
Data quality programs are needed when databases are first created.	Data quality programs are an ongoing investment that requires collaboration across businesses, with IT, operations and even external partners.
Measuring data quality errors is enough.	Measuring all aspects of data management is required.
Data quality means the same thing to every process and every organization.	Data quality requirements are different across processes. You can't assume quality with data; you must establish requirements for it, then measure.
Data quality is someone else's job and really only belongs to those whose job it is to manage it.	Every person who touches data has a role to play in improving its quality and ensuring that is managed effectively.

Identifying Your Audience

Let's assume that you've garnered support from top executives. Next, there are three other groups across the company you need to address. An important job for anyone who must lead a data management initiative is to quickly segment those individuals, whose support you need, into these three groups:

1. Those who get it immediately; those who understand the value of data management.
2. Those who don't get it but may eventually; those who have responsibilities that depend on data management, but may not know that they need to support these efforts.
3. Those who don't get it and never will; those who truly don't understand why investments in time and resources should be made in this efforts.

Once segmented, the strategy for winning over these groups is simple:

- For those who get it, recruit them into your ranks immediately. Make them your evangelists. Call on them often to tell their success stories, herald their successes in your presentations, and recognize them as heroes. Look for these individuals throughout the organization—they are "Friends of Data."

- For those who don't get it but may eventually, begin a structured and systematic education program. The Chief Data Officer should launch a broad company education program as discussed in the previous chapter. For individuals leading department or function-level data initiatives, the education can be tailored to the specific organization. Teach this group about the benefits of

Exhibit 12.2. Segmenting Your Audience

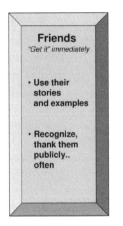
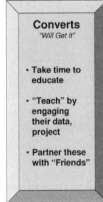

Friends
"Get it" immediately

• Use their stories and examples

• Recognize, thank them publicly.. often

Converts
"Will Get It"

• Take time to educate

• "Teach" by engaging their data, project

• Partner these with "Friends"

Ludites
"Never will get it"

• Contain their influence

• Communicate data improvements from other areas

• Engage executive management sponsor

data management. Instruct them on the how's and why's of good data quality processes. Use their processes as examples. Make the lessons short and specific to their jobs. Make sure that lessons are convenient to take and easily understood. Use your evangelists to help you with this instruction. It gives them visibility and supports your cause. Once this group has completed training, they are your "Data Converts."

• Last we have the "Ludites," or the enemies of data. These are the individuals within the organization that don't understand why this is important and may never. Oftentimes this group consists not only of those managers who don't have the time or see the importance, but it may also contain those who have tried data quality initiatives in the past and failed. Your approach here depends on your own organization and personal preference. The most important thing to do with this group is to make sure that they don't distract from your efforts. As long as their skepticism is contained and managed, you can continue to evangelize and sell the concepts of data management to your executive management. Pinpointing these individuals early and neutralizing them is very important to your success. But be wary; they do not always initially look, talk or act like people who will be distracters or naysayers. When these individuals populate the executive ranks of your organization, you have a unique challenge. Here you must work actively to surround them with positive energy, prepare for the negative backlash and neutralize all negativity about maintaining data.

When the naysayer exists in the executive ranks, you have a unique challenge. Take some advice from others who have faced similar challenges. For example, Texas Instruments was in the software business for a few years with a tool called IEF, Information Engineering Facility. This tool was revolutionary in that it completely shifted the application development cycle from 20% planning/80% coding to 80% planning/20% coding. In other words, it changed the way software developers in large organizations develop software and that caused a tremendous challenge to TI's sales organization. Not only did the sales representatives have to sell a new product, but they had to convince organizations that bought the product to change the way they developed software. No small feat. What the marketing team did was unusual for a high tech company, but something that consumer companies have long employed: Highlight your users. Texas Instruments began to highlight in advertising and events those "brave thought leaders" who were embracing this new way of developing in-house application software. It worked. By spotlighting those who bought and used the product with success, others began trying it. Within a year, a majority of those highlighted in advertising success stories were promoted to new positions within their own companies where they had been heralded as "change agents." And success bred success. When TI started mentioning that leaders in this area were getting promoted from their application development jobs to CIO and beyond, sales skyrocketed. CIOs are people, too. Those who hadn't yet tried automated software development were eager to try it, to position themselves and their organizations as innovative.

The most important thing to remember when working with the group that does not support your efforts initially is: Don't spend all of your resources on their conversion. It is often easy to find yourself committing people, time and dollars to help with "pilots" or presentation after presentation on data quality. You must determine whether this activity is moving your cause forward or is simply activity for the sake of activity. The process of determining who presents an obstacle and neutralizing them can take time. Be patient. Determining the motivation of this group is the key.

Dealing with Resistance— The Chief Data Officer's Challenge

A Chief Data Officer has unique challenges if her peers or other key senior executives of the company resist change. However, as with all large change efforts, resistance is inevitable and can be overcome. Here are some reasons you might encounter resistance:

1. Lack of understanding
2. Disagreement with the data strategy or specific approach
3. Disagreement with the severity of the issue
4. Disagreement over who "owns" fixing the problem
5. Lack of resources
6. Lack of funds
7. Other business priorities
8. All of the above

Ignoring the resistance from an influential constituent or stakeholder is not an option. The Chief Data Officer needs to be prepared to address the resistance quickly. The following guidelines might be helpful.

The easiest resistance to address is that which stems from lack of understanding. If you work from the premise that "reasonable people come to reasonable conclusions when given all the facts," you have the appropriate attitude for facing this type of resistance. Take these steps:

- Schedule one-on-one conversations that explain the data management strategy, its end state, your approach and how and why this is important.
- Allow for multiple sessions in a setting that encourages questions and debates. Repeat as often as necessary until the strategy is well understood.

Addressing resistance that comes from disagreement with the strategy, approach, severity or ownership of the issue is best defused with facts—clear, concise, irrefutable facts. Facts that describe the existing data issues in quantifiable terms are the best way to soften this kind of resistance. Here are a few examples of those kinds of facts:

- Data quality metrics showing the overall completeness, validity or accuracy of data important to this constituent's department
- Numbers that show the impact of data customer metrics such as revenue or customer satisfaction, or numbers that show a loss of productivity or additional expense

Resistance to data initiatives because of limited resources, funds or time is best addressed with a helping hand. This type of resistance is best addressed by the CDO providing "loaner" skills or start-up dollars to fund data management activities in the individual businesses. Making it clearly understood that dollars and resources are for a limited time is an imperative. Your goal is to get the resisting organization and executive to staff and resource data initiatives at their required level in the future.

Resistance because of "other priorities" may require some senior-level help. This type of resistance is often most difficult because it may ultimately require intervention from the CDO's boss. If resistance is coming from other executives who have been given other priorities, it's difficult to make an impact without senior-level interference. Exhausting all other options before turning to the CEO is the best course of action. Realize, too, that the excuse for not making progress on data initiatives because of "other priorities" often masks hidden agendas. Ferreting out the hidden agenda requires patience, open communication and political savvy.

The most dangerous resistance comes from an executive who says all the right things about data, data management and quality, but who always fails to step up to the issues of funding, governance and usage. Here is where you will face the last

Exhibit 12.3. Resistance "Busters"

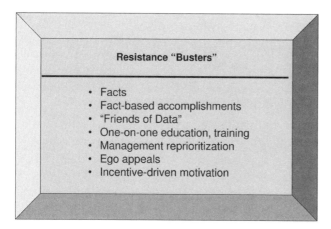

Resistance "Busters"

- Facts
- Fact-based accomplishments
- "Friends of Data"
- One-on-one education, training
- Management reprioritization
- Ego appeals
- Incentive-driven motivation

great challenge—how to create a space for your efforts to exist within his or her organization. Bottom line: appeal to their greed. Most executives, no matter their position, are motivated by some form of incentive—salary, stock, title, a corner office, the key to the executive washroom. You can name all the benefits that would motivate you and you can probably find a great commonality. How to link data management to those initiatives that executive cares about is your challenge.

Selling the Benefits of Data Management

To think like an executive, think like a salesperson. That simply means: (1) start with an objective, (2) create a sales plan, (3) handle objections and (4) make the sale. Let's look at each of these tasks in turn.

Start with an Objective

Every salesperson worth his commission knows exactly what his goal is for the year and what he has to do to make it. In selling executives on the benefits of data management, your goal should be numbers just like the salesperson's. For you, however, consider that your "number" is a percentage of the overall number of managers and executives that you have to convert. For example, let's assume that there are five major executives in your company who handle finance, marketing, sales, product development and operations. Working for each of them are six managers who have considerable span of control and make most of the decisions in your company. So you can see immediately that the total population that you must educate and "sell" on data management is thirty. Let's also assume, for the sake of easy math, that your group of executives and managers break out evenly into groups of ten when you evaluate them and then segment them on whether they are receptive or not to data management issues. You conveniently should end up with ten executives and managers who "get it," ten who can and ten who you should work on minimizing their

Exhibit 12.4. Making the "Data Sale"

impact on your projects. If you put that into a salesperson's language, you now have ten hot prospects and ten who should go into your pipeline.

There are goals for how many people you need to convert and then there are goals for your data management efforts as well. Make sure that you keep both of these in mind.

Every good sales plan has a way of measuring whether it was successful or not. The ultimate measure of sales is the revenue related. In selling an idea, often the best measure of how successful you are comes also in the form of a dollar. In this case, however, an executive's investment in resources to support your efforts is a sign that you've successfully sold the idea of data management. Don't become disheartened if what you get is people instead of money. Getting any kind of support that costs an executive either time or money is very valuable and should be considered as a sign of success. As in every successful sales plan, however, you need to set yourself a goal and make sure that your key executives know how much it will take. You may not always get that amount, but no one will accuse you of not being clear about your intentions.

Create a Sales Plan

With your goal in mind, start with the actions that you consider most important for "selling" your hottest prospects, those who may already understand your mission. From our analysis above, there are ten of those managers and executives who you must make evangelists for your cause, business decision-making based on solid, good-quality data.

Write down your sales plan and keep track of the progress you're making with each executive. It also helps to write down the key messages about your data management initiative to ensure that when you communicate, you are always driving home these key messages. For example, if you're trying to make sure that you secure funding for your initiatives by a particular time, say for next year's budget, you may need to make sure that you drive a sense of urgency into your communications.

Your sales plan should be simple. Here's a quick outline:

1. Schedule time with each manager to make sure that they understand what your goals are and how you plan on achieving them. (We talk about executive dashboards and the numbers that you'll need to manage them Chapter 4.)

2. Develop an easy-to-communicate, easy-to-understand presentation that outlines:
   - What they know or don't know about data and how it flows through their organization
   - What challenges they face and how data can either minimize or eliminate the challenge or issue
   - What they could gain by being supportive of a data management initiative

3. Deliver your presentation to each executive and to his direct reports and answer all questions that they may have.

4. Make sure that you send out regular communications about the achievements of your team and update all your evangelists on how you are progressing toward your goals. Here's some quick communication advice:
   - Make it simple, but consistent. Touch-base meetings, short emails about successes you're seeing or quick phone messages that give a heads-up tone to challenges are methods to consider when striving for recognition of the data management efforts.
   - Relate the communication to something that is of interest to them. Your goal is to have them adopt your data management initiative and when they do, make it their own.
   - Make it easy for them to get information about your initiative from sources other than you, such as Web sites or other organizations' executives. This is where you can use your executive ambassadors most effectively.
   - Schedule periodic and regular meetings to discuss the progress made by the data management efforts. Be sure to always relate any progress to their specific organizations.
   - Decide what messages are key to your success and keep communicating them consistently with different media and different approaches. If you're trying to initiate a corporate culture change, you've got to be sure that you constantly show examples of successful change.

In your selling process, make sure that you don't lose sight of the value of educating executives on data management and why it is important to their business. Seek opportunities to share with them key insights from successful initiatives; view the chance as a way to educate. Share with them what other companies are doing, what outside consultants and your customers are doing in this area, how the competition is doing it better. Educating an executive most often requires an outside-in focus. They respond much better to what the market, the competition and their customers are doing. How you and your teams are managing inside is of much lower priority.

In addition to constituent-specific selling plans, companywide selling programs are also helpful. These include:

1. **Internal communication and PR strategy.** Address the "why and what" of enterprise data management through:
   - Newsletter
   - Internal Web sites
   - Companywide meetings
   - Town halls meetings for individual organizations

   In a PR campaign, consider using tag lines or catchy phrases that are easy understand but get the message across. For example:
   - Like a good neighbor, Data is there!
   - Data Quality Matters!
   - Providing Data You can Trust
   - Ask not what data can do for you, but what you can do for data!

2. **Storytelling.** Collect stories of data management successes as well as stories where customers were significantly impacted because of insufficient or deficient data management. One company story told of a long-time customer who started receiving hundreds of incorrect mail pieces at her home. When her personal address had been changed in the company database, it had incorrectly been identified with a prominent government agency!

3. **Education.** Address the "how" with formal and informal education. Explain how data can be handled, designed or changed by following good data management principles. Consider making these classes mandatory for all new employees.

4. **Recognition systems.** Often the best way to motivate is to reward or recognize efforts. Recognition, however, can be used to highlight both the good and the bad. Here are some ways:

   Rewards for compliance
   - Establish reward systems for meeting enterprise data management goals.
   - Ensure yearly performance evaluations include data management responsibilities.
   - Tie company bonuses to meeting data quality targets.

Penalties for noncompliance
- Noncompliance reflected in audits made public to all departments and that carry performance evaluation and salary implications.
- Public ranging systems or contests. These can broadly communicate where each department or organization stands on data management. The "rack 'um and stack 'um" approach plays to the competitive spirit inherent in all individuals.
- Waivers. Noncompliance could be addressed by giving the organization a "waiver" for noncompliance, but only for a period of time. This gives the organization time to fix any noncompliance issues and also sends a message to the organization that the Chief Data Officer is flexible, but firm.

Handle Objections

Handling objections is the least favorite part of any salesperson's job. But handling objections well is just as important as communicating well your objectives and plans. You will face objections. From your first group of evangelists, the objections should be fairly straightforward and easy to handle. Remember, you selected this group because of they already "got it." Their objections will be framed around those things that make them successful in business. Most will be concerned about how these data management efforts will generate revenue, grow the business or create shareholder value for the company. Your objectives should plainly fall into one of these three categories or, preferably, *all* three.

Other objections that you should be prepared to handle will probably have more to do with the specific area of business your evangelist represents. Finance managers will worry about how these efforts will affect their numbers or their planning cycles. Sales managers may voice concerns about how these efforts will impact sales productivity. And, manufacturing may be concerned for how data management will help them with inventory. Whatever concerns these different areas have must be dealt with effectively by your data management initiatives. Your evangelists must see improvements in their areas of responsibility for them to be true believers and apostles for your cause.

Don't despair. These efforts will take time. The average data management initiative begins with a scope of two to three years. You'll be most successful if you can engage a few of your evangelists early with your initiatives and show quick wins. Using these "wins" as success stories will help you sell into the other groups—one by one.

Ask for the Sale

And finally, all good salespeople know that "asking for the order" is a necessity. Just because you're getting good signs that an executive understands data management, appreciates what it can do for his or her organization and thinks it's a positive thing, doesn't mean that you'll get funding or resources. You'll have to ask for that.

When you do ask for the order, be specific. "I need a full-time, data management-trained resource for the next two years. I would monetize that at a $300K investment from your team." This is a much better approach than saying you need data management support. Most executives can "support" you without giving you dollars or resources—or at least they believe they can.

Remember, this first sales plan was intended to help you with the first group that you need to sell—those that "get it." Once you have a solid base of believers who are helping you spread the word about data management, you may find that the next group is more easily converted. Throughout all of these efforts, you may have to deal with those who will try to detract from your efforts oftentimes because they don't clearly understand the benefits of your efforts. One of the most successful salespeople that we ever met was once asked how she managed to be so successful, often outperforming her colleagues by 10 to 1. She clearly articulated that her first task always was to determine if the prospect had the budget to pay for her product. (In your case, you need to assess if the prospect has the ability and desire to invest in data management.) When asked what she did when the prospect clearly did not have the funding, she was quick to declare: "I simply say to myself, '*NEXT.*' I don't waste my time with those who can't buy." Above all, this is the most important lesson as you strive to build a data management program. Don't waste your time with those who can't or won't help you.

Summary

In Chapter 6, Margaret became a "Friend of Data." Caroline leveraged Margaret's success to "sell" data quality to Ed, the VP of Manufacturing. In her discussion with Ed, Margaret shared not just her results but her initial personal reservations to the project and her resource challenges. She made it real for Ed. Ed was more receptive, but not totally convinced. Still, he agreed to pilot a data quality project and assign resources from his shop.

Caroline assigned one of her best data quality specialist to work with Ed's team. She also privately provided one-on-one education to Ed on how other companies handled these manufacturing problems. In time, Ed became a "convert." Caroline now had two data management success stories. Better yet, the business data stewards for sales and manufacturing emerged from Margaret and Ed's organization.

Both Ed and Margaret went on to develop ongoing data quality programs that resulted in cost reductions and increased sales for the company. When the company acquired XYZ Corporation, Margaret, Ed and Caroline were assigned to the integration team. Because of their data management program and the business data stewardship expertise, the sales and manufacturing data integration was completed ahead of schedule. However, the integration of the employee and product data had significant implementation issues and delays. This ultimately convinced the CEO that data management was critical for the company. Caroline "asked for the order." She seized the opportunity to name data stewards for Employee and Product data with full support from the CEO. She also received funding for rolling out an enterprise data management program for the entire company. Now Caroline had her sale. She changed the culture by demonstrating success in stages with her "converts and friends" and seizing an important business problem to fix!

INDEX

A

Address standardization, 109
Asset inventory, 75–79
Asset management, 90–91
Attitudes, changing about data, 144–47

B

"Bad data", 59–64, 107
Bank of International Settlement (BIS), 23
BASEL Committee on Banking Supervision,
    22, 23
BASEL standards, 22–23
Behaviors, 46, 56
Belonging needs, 47, 51–52
Black Belt, 89
BPM applications, 31–34
Business data steward forum, 134, 135
Business data stewards, 107, 110, 111,
    122–32. *See also* Information
    management professionals
  appointing, 122, 130
  attributes of, 128
  mission of, 124–28
  need for, 122–24
  success steps, 130
  reporting options, 129
  training, 131–32
Business objectives, data that affects, 4–5
Business performance management (BPM),
    31–44
  BPM applications, 31–33
  data challenges, 33–34
  data management and, 42–44
  ways to implement, 34–42

Business processes
  correlation to data issues, 65, 67
  role in data accuracy, 5, 6, 7
Business-to-business companies,
  compliance and, 17, 18

C

CAN-SPAM, 24
Center for Media Research, 82
CEO, role in BPM success, 36. *See also*
  Executive sponsorship
Certification programs, for IM
  professionals, 142–43
Certified Information Security Auditor
  (CISA), 20
Chief data officer (CDO), 114–121
  case for, , 114–15
  reporting options, 119–20
  responsibilities of, 116–17
  skills of, 117–19
  success measures, 121
Children's Online Privacy Protection Act
  (COPPA), 24
Choice Point, 27
Clancy, Kevin, 3
Committee of Sponsoring Organizations
  (COSO), 29
Communication
  importance in BPM success, 39
  role in changing attitudes, 151, 152,
Company strategy, tying to information
  programs, 69
Compliance, 16–30

data management and, 18–20
data privacy and, 23–27
financial reporting and, 28–30
information security and, 19, 20–23
risk management and, 20–21
Compliance rules, for metadata, 84, 90
Confidentiality, 19–20
Consumer companies, compliance and, 17,
    18
Control Objectives for Information and
    Related Technology (COBIT), 21
Controls, for data protection, 111–12
Corporate data organization, 135
Covey, Stephen, 11, 56
Critical data, determining, 4–5, 85
Customer, how data reflects, 11–15
Customer data, valuing, 85–86
Customer experience, leveraging, 69

D

Data
    as scapegoat, 4, 5
    as vital sign, 1
    changing attitudes about, 144–47
    characteristics of, 6–7
    decay of, 104, 106–07
    importance of, 1–2
    managers' disbelief of, 3–4
    ways to create effectively, 7–8
    ways to evaluate trustworthiness of, 8–10
Data, as company asset, 74–91
    asset inventory, 75–79
    asset management, 90–91
    data asset value, 85–88
    enterprise metadata repository, 79–80
    metadata benefits, 81–83
    metadata owner, 80–81, 84, 85
    policies, , 89–90
Data, customer view and, 11–15
Data assets
    classifying, 76–78
    describing, 78
    determining cost of, 86
    determining quality of, 79
    determining value of, 85–88

managing, 90
Data asset value, 85–88
Data availability, 20
Data converts, 146
Data crisis, as way to get management
    attention, 68–69
Data culture, 45–56
    data needs, 48–53
    human needs, 45–47, 52
    steps to implement, 54–56
DataFlux, 12
Data governance, 132–34, 135
    processes for metadata, 84, 85, 90–91
    role in BPM success, 41–42
Data governance office, 134
Data issues
    correlation to business processes and, 65,
        67
    new systems and, 95–99, 102
    re-engineering projects and, 97
    scattered data and, 99–100
    uncovering, 93–95
Data management
    business performance management and,
        42–44
    compliance and, 18–20
    data privacy and, 27
    future of, 137–38
    information security and, 23
    role of executives in, 65, 65–73
Data management program
    attitudes about, 144–47
    challenges, 147–49
    policies, 88–90
    roles in, 88–89
    selling benefits of149–53
Data management scorecard   137
Data mart, 78
Data needs, ways to explain to executives
    12
Data object, 124
Data privacy, 23–27, 110–12
    data management and, 27
    laws governing, 24–27
Data profiling, 109
Data quality,

defined, 101
investment in, 92, 93
as IT responsibility, 104–06
maintenance of, 107–08
management of, 106–07
myths about, 102–04,
Data standardization, 109
Data stewards. *See* Business data stewards
Data warehouse, 78
Deficiency needs, 46
"Dirty" data, 76, 77
Dresner, Howard, 31
Dun & Bradstreet, 106

E

Education, role in changing attitudes,
      145–46
Employee data, valuing, 86
Enemies of data, 146
English, Larry, 122
Enron, 16, 27
Enterprise data management program, 50,
      51, 52, 53, 54, 92–113
   data myths, 102–04
   data quality, 101–02
   data quality management, 106–07
   data quality maintenance, 107–08
   IT department and, 65, 104–06
   reliability needs, 93–101
   starting point, 92–93, 108–10
   security needs, 110–12
Enterprise metadata repository, 43, 79–85
   accessibility of, 85
   benefits of, 81–83
   updating of, 84–85
   obstacles to, 83–85
   owner of, 80–81, 84
Esteem needs, 47, 52–53
Executive dashboard, 38–41
   automated input, 38–39
   drill-down capabilities, 39
   operational meetings, 40–41
   presentation options, 40
Executive forum, 132–34
Executive sponsor, at belonging stage, 52

Executive sponsorship, 65–73
   importance of, 65–66
   ways to get, 68–73
External data, quality problems and, 100,
      101

F

Fayyad, Usama, 115
Federal Financial Institution Examination
      Council (FFIEC), 21
Financial consequences, of noncompliance,
      16, 17
Financial privacy rule, 26
Financial reporting, 16
   data implications and, 29–30
   laws governing, 28–29
Forrester Research, 69
Frankland, David, 69
Friends of data, 145

G

Gartner Group, 18, 31, 84, 105
Gidley, Scott, 12
Goals, as way to get management attention,
      72–73
Gramm-Leach Bliley Act (GLBA), 26

H

Harrah's, 69
Health Insurance Portability and
      Accountability Act (HIPAA), 24
Hierarchy of data needs, 48–53
   belonging needs, 51–52
   esteem needs, 42–53
   physical needs, 48–49
   safety needs, 49–50
   self-actualization needs, 53
Hierarchy of human needs, 45–47, 52. *See
      also* Maslow, Abraham
   belonging needs, 47
   esteem needs, 47
   physical needs, 46
   safety needs, 46–47
   self-actualization needs, 47

I

IBM, 69, 106
Information, as "utility service", 69–72
Information assets
  documenting construction of, 78–79
  identifying, 75–76
Information engineering facility (IEF) tool, 146–47
Information integrity, 20
Information management maturity assessment, 135–37
Information management professionals 139–42. *See also* Business data steward
  certification programs for, 142–43
  skills of, 140–41
Information programs, tying to company strategy, 69
Information security
  compliance and, 19–20
  data management and, 23
  risk management and, 20–21
Information Security Forum, 22
Information Security Forum Standard of Good Practice, 22
Information security levels, 110
Information security organization, 111, 112
International Data Corporation (IDC), 82
ISO/IEC 17799, 22
IT department, as custodian of data quality, 65, 104–06

J

Japan's Personal Information Protection Act, 26

K

Key performance indicators (KPIs), 37, 42, 43
Krieg, Peter, 3
Knightbridge, 33

L

Legislation, 19, 21–23
Lillien, Gary, 4

Linking, 109

M

Maslow, Abraham, 45, 46, 48. *See also* Hierarchy of human needs
Master data, 77–78
Matching, 109
Mental models, 4, 66. *See also* Objective decision models *and* Subjective decision models
Metadata technology, selecting, 84
Metric definitions, importance in BPM success, 38
Monitoring, 109
Monster.com, 139
Motivation, 46
Myths, about data quality, 102–04

N

New systems, data problems and, 95–99, 102
Noncompliance, financial consequences of, 16, 17
Non-public information (NPI), 86
Numbers, management's disbelief of , 3–4

O

Objective decision models, 4. *See also* Mental models *and* Subjective decision models
Operational data store (ODS), 77

P

Payment Card Industry Data Security Standard, 25–26
Performance measurement. *See* Business performance management
Physical needs, 46, 48–49
PricewaterhouseCoopers, 93
Privacy, 16
Product data, valuing, 86
Production data, 112

R

Rangaswamy, Arvind, 4
Re-engineering projects, data problems and, 97
Regulatory compliance, 16, 18, 19
Relationships, building in data culture, 52, 103
Reports, 11
Residual risks, 21
Resistance, to data management changes, 147–49
Return-on-asset metrics, 86
Risk, 20
Risk management, 20–21

S

Safeguard rule, 26
Safe Harbor, 24–25
Safety needs, 46–47, 49–50
Sarbanes-Oxley Act (SOX), 28, 33, 69
SB 1386–California Civil Code, 27
Scattered data, data problems and, 99–100
Self-actualization needs, 47, 53
Self-service data, 137
Six Sigma, 89
Standards, 21–23
Subjective decision models, 4. *See also* Mental models *and* Objective decision models

T

TDAN.com, 117
Texas Instruments (TI), 146–47
The Data Warehousing Institute (TDWI) , 33, 36, 42, 142
Threat, 20
360-degree view, 11–15
  barriers to, 13–15
T J Maxx, 17, 18
TJX Corporation, 17–18
Trusted sources, 44

U

Unstructured data assets, 78
USA Patriot Act, 27

V

Vulnerability, 20

W

Wells, David, 142
WorldCom, 16, 27

Y

Yahoo, 115

Racom Communications Order Form

QUANTITY	TITLE	PRICE	AMOUNT
_____	*Managing Your Business Data,* **Theresa Kushner/Maria Villar**	$32.95	_____
_____	*Media Strategt and Planning Workbook,* **DL Dickinson**	$24.95	_____
_____	*Marketing Metrics in Action,* **Laura Patterson**	$24.95	_____
_____	The *IMC Handbook,* **J. Stephen Kelly/Susna K. Jones**	$27.95	_____
_____	*Print Matters,* **Randall Hines/Robert Lauterborn**	$27.95	_____
_____	*The Business of Database Marketing,* **Richard N. Tooker**	$49.95	_____
_____	*Customer Churn, Retention, and Profitability,* **Arthur Middleton Hughes**	$44.95	_____
_____	*Data-Driven Business Models,* **Alan Weber**	$49.95	_____
_____	*Creative Strategy in Direct & Interactive Marketing,* **Susan K. Jones**	$49.95	_____
_____	*Branding Iron,* **Charlie Hughes and William Jeanes**	$27.95	_____
_____	*Managing Sales Leads,* **James Obermayer**	$39.95	_____
_____	*Creating the Marketing Experience,* **Joe Marconi**	$49.95	_____
_____	*Coming to Concurrence,* **J. Walker Smith/Ann Clurman/Craig Wood**	$34.95	_____
_____	*Brand Babble: Sense and Nonsense about Branding,* **Don E. Schultz/Heidi F. Schultz**	$24.95	_____
_____	*The New Marketing Conversation,* **Donna Baier Stein/Alexandra MacAaron**	$34.95	_____
_____	*Trade Show and Event Marketing,* **Ruth Stevens**	$59.95	_____
_____	*Sales & Marketing 365,* **James Obermayer**	$17.95	_____
_____	*Accountable Marketing,* **Peter J. Rosenwald**	$59.95	_____
_____	*Contemporary Database Marketing,* **Martin Baier/Kurtis Ruf/G. Chakraborty**	$89.95	_____
_____	*Catalog Strategist's Toolkit,* **Katie Muldoon**	$59.95	_____
_____	*Marketing Convergence,* **Susan K. Jones/Ted Spiegel**	$34.95	_____
_____	*High-Performance Interactive Marketing,* **Christopher Ryan**	$39.95	_____
_____	*Public Relations: The Complete Guide,* **Joe Marconi**	$49.95	_____
_____	*The Marketer's Guide to Public Relations,* **Thomas L. Harris/Patricia T. Whalen**	$39.95	_____
_____	*The White Paper Marketing Handbook,* **Robert W. Bly**	$39.95	_____
_____	*Business-to-Business Marketing Research,* **Martin Block/Tamara Block**	$69.95	_____
_____	*Hot Appeals or Burnt Offerings,* **Herschell Gordon Lewis**	$24.95	_____
_____	*On the Art of Writing Copy,* **Herschell Gordon Lewis**	$34.95	_____
_____	*Open Me Now,* **Herschell Gordon Lewis**	$21.95	_____
_____	*Marketing Mayhem,* **Herschell Gordon Lewis**	$39.95	_____
_____	*Asinine Advertising,* **Herschell Gordon Lewis**	$22.95	_____
_____	*The Ultimate Guide To Purchasing Website, Video, Print & Other Creative Services,* **Bobbi Balderman**	$18.95	_____

FORTHCOMING—Reserve your copy now. Send no money. We'll notify you when your copy is off the press.

QUANTITY	TITLE	PRICE	AMOUNT
_____	Debra Wilson Ellis, *Multichannel Marketing*	$39.95	_____
_____	Arthur Hughes, *Successful Email Marketing Methods*	$59.95	_____
_____	John Goodman, *Retail Database Marketing*	$49.95	_____
_____	Don Schultz/Reg Price, *Reliability Rules*	$29.95	_____
_____	Weber/Sander/van Boel, *Marketing Trigger*	$39.95	_____

Name/Title_____

Company _____

Street Address _____

City/State/Zip _____

Email _____ Phone _____

Credit Card: ☐ VISA ☐ MasterCard
              ☐ American Express ☐ Discover

☐ Check or money order enclosed (payable to Racom Communications in U.S. dollars drawn on a U.S. bank)

Subtotal	_____
Subtotal from other side	_____
8.65% Tax	_____
Shipping & Handling	_____
$7.00 for first book; $1.00 for each additional book.	
TOTAL	_____

Number _____ Exp. Date _____

Signature _____